Decoding Nigeria Imperialist Agenda

Audacity of Nigerian Political Revolution

*Decoding the Imperialist Agenda

*Deliverance of the Crippled giant of Africa

• 10 Reasons for this Revolution

• Letter to Nigerian Terrorists

Emmanuel Adetula

To order additional copies of this book,

CONTACT Emmanuel Adetula

Nigeria Contact: TULALUM HOUSE: G.P.O. BOX 15121, IBADAN, OYO STATE—NIGERIA *tulalum@yahoo.com*

USA Contact: CCN HOUSE: P.O.BOX 111589, LOS ANGELES, CA. 90011 *ccnhouse@sbcglobal.net* **(310) 292-1147**

Website contact: Make $100 donation to CCN Center for Peace and receive this book free with my other 3 books from Emmanuel Adetula . *www.emmanueltula.com*

AUTHORITY TO REPRODUCE THIS BOOK

CONTENTS

NIGERIA POLITICIANS AND THEIR FIVE MASTERS 9

DECODING THE CODES of the name "NIGERIA" 12

MAKING FEAR TO BECOME AFRAID 17

LETTER TO NIGERIAN TERRORISTS 22

AFRICA IS A GUN, NIGERIA IS THE TRIGGER 31

THE IDEOLOGY OF THIS REVOLUTION 34

TEN REASONS WHY I ACCEPTED THE LEADERSHIP
OF THIS REVOLUTION

REASONS ONE FOR THIS REVOLUTION 41

REASON TWO FOR THIS REVOLUTION 44

REASON THREE FOR THIS REVOLUTION 48

REASON FOUR FOR THIS REVOLUTION 53

REASON FIVE FOR THIS REVOLUTION 55

REASON SIX FOR THIS REVOLUTION 57

REASON SEVEN FOR THIS REVOLUTION 59

REASON EIGHT FOR THIS REVOLUTION 61

REASON NINE FOR THIS REVOLUTION 64

THE SPIRITUAL ALEGORY OF THIS REVOLUTION 69

OLUSEGUN OBASANJO & USMAN YAR`ADUA 74

NIGERIANS CHRISTIANS 80

THE PRAYER OF CHAIRMAN TULA 85

Nigeria Politicians AND THEIRFiveMASTERS

You know, I know, everybody in *leadership* knows that truth is not enough to win in governance, particularly when you are destined to change the attitude, character and disposition of a legitimate Christianity and Islamic religious mafia, or the established culture of the people and the monarchial establishment that has existed over 5000 years before you are born, an establishment that are more powerful than any elected person to run Nigeria government, because these establishment are rooted in the perpetual legacy of Nigeria imperialist masters whose legacy for Nigeria social and economic advancement are perpetuated by the western media employees who are paid by their boss to use media propaganda as the super power weapon of warfare to put Nigeria and Nigerians down as corrupt. internet scams artists. Dishonest and terrorists.

And what shall we say then, if the west and Nigeria media is not for us, who shall not be against revolution? but the people of Nigerian, despite the antagonistic posture of some News Editors of major Nigerian Radio, Television and Newspapers who are trained in the school of western media propaganda, negative reporting about this movement of the people, we shall overcome. Despite the fact that all Nigeria political leadership operates under the control of the western media and Nigeria press boys and girls to perpetuate an age long agenda, we shall overcome, despite the fact that the media believe that there is no single Nigerian alive that is not corrupt, we shall overcome, despite the fact that some Nigeria press boys and girls has become a complete idiot in 2010 and are clueless about the imperialist masters codes to rule Nigeria with a remote control using media propaganda as their weapon of welfare to stop Nigeria socio-political and economy advancement, I say again. that we shall overcome.

Nigeria press has moved itself above the ladder, and has abandoned its role as the fourth power of the realms to one of the master of the Executive and legislative arms of Nigeria government, Nigeria press girls with lipstick are no longer the watchdog for the people of Nigeria, but are now drunk and intoxicated with negative news reporting that are feed to them through the internet by the western media, to position Nigeria media as one of the five masters of Nigerian politicians, I say, we shall overcome, Nigeria media is no more on the side of the Nigerian people but has now become the enemy of Nigeria freedom by their alliance with the western media propaganda warfare against Nigerians in Diaspora and the Nigerian political leadership. I say, we shall overcome, Therefore the kind of lazy news gathering system, despite lack of the tools for investigative journalism and un-inform mindset of the press boys and girls who learnt nothing in college than English grammar that has taken over Nigeria media, I say we shall overcome, despite the negative news reporting and false story telling of the Nigeria press against the leaders of this revolution, Here say, we shall overcome, despite the fact that some news editors of Nigeria media who have taken position themselves as monopoly of wisdom because they can speak and write very well in English language to rule our land, and that anybody who speak no English is not fit to rule our land. We have come to tell them, we shall overcome. Because this revolution has come to revoke the certificate of occupancy of the Queen plantation that is located around the Niger river area, and give the land back to the original owner with immediate effect, and the people of Niger river area says, let my people go, and let the freedom rain. Let it rain, let it rain.

Nigerian Politicians has five masters, the religious leaders, the traditional rulers, the soldiers who turn politicians, the western world leaders using the west and Nigeria media boys and girls.

All the elected person in government got to positions of political leadership through identification, endorsement or sponsorship from one or more of these five establishment, if so, how do you manage the social political economy of a nation to benefit 140 million people if you have these five Supervisors?. You either choose to make the 140 million people your boss or run the government to satisfy your only 5 boss and remain defiant to the people needs. At least you and your family belongs to the 10 % of the population who are shielded or protected from experiencing poverty like the rest 90% of Nigerian people.

I do not enjoy writing this book or take this responsibility for myself, this is against my desire or wishes, I am writing this book right now in my vacation resort, where the pacific ocean can be seen miles away from my living room sliding doors, and the water of the ocean is splashing and occasionally drops the water of pacific ocean to my bedroom window, therefore I can live the rest of my life here in United States, not minding if all of you over there in Nigeria lives under $1 a day, But God gave me this assignment and I have to obey him, imagine if God placed this load on your own head like he did to me right now, what would you do? Would you cut your head off, this assignment was squeezed from my life experiences as a Citizen of Nigeria for over 30 years, and in Diaspora now as a Resident in United States in the last 12 years, my soul was squeezed to the last drop of my soul, like a man trying to get juice from an orange and what flows out of my soul people is the liquid that was used as ink to load the fountain pen that I used to write this book.

I say the truth in God, I lie not, my conscience also bearing me witness, that I have great heaviness and continual sorrow in my heart for being elected by God to stand in the gap for my kinsmen and my people of Nigeria, therefore I am writing this book because a necessity is laid upon me by a supernatural forces too much for me to ignore, and I wish I am like you Nigerians in Diaspora who is free to get involved in this kind of Nigerian politics, but has concerns yourself with making money and join the 10% Nigerians at the top making a better life for your own family and care less about what happen to the rest 90% of the people over there in Nigeria, you removed your wife and children from Nigerian and file for citizenship of another country, but since I am not you guys, I will be me. I am that I am, therefore I have agreed with a big ego, big ideas, big dream, big plan, God's grace and a huge luck to be one of the leader of Nigeria revolution not because I want a material compensation for doing this service to my people. But because there is a spiritual allegory behind this my assignment in Nigeria. Nobody alive can take this position for him or she if God did not sent him.

Having accepted the leadership of this revolution let me make it clear that I will report to no Traditional rulers, to no Religious leaders, and to no super powers in this revolution, but only to the power of Nigerian people. Nonetheless this revolution shall have a decent respect to the opinion of mankind and it owes a debt to ancient Greece, and Rome and to European civilization and the principle of United states history to work towards complete separation of Churches and the state, separation of Islam and Sharia laws from the state, the sanctity of civil and human rights of all Nigerians. In shall Allah.

Decoding THE CODES

of the name "Nigeria"

The code of Nigeria name can is taken from the bible according to Exodus 1: 9-22. And the imperialists said, come on now, let us deal wisely with these local indigene in Niger river area, because they are numerous in number, very strong, intelligent and smart individuals, lets deal with them wisely, lest they multiply in numbers, and with their natural capability of doing things, they may rise up in economic and political power and in technological advancement, nuke power, and the Islam believers among them which consist about 65 percent may team up with the Islamic east and join the Arabs and fight against us, and so let's get the wise among them, get them educated in our own land. and teach them our western culture, make some as immigrants in our own land and the rest go back home to rule their land with English language and inject in them our own culture, among them let us plant disease of malaria, polio, tuberculosis and HIV to kill their children in infancy to reduce their population that is rising with a speed of light.

When the wise and educated among them cry foul, we would create a donor and loan program for them, to help them, by this system they will remain in debt to us forever, and we continue to ship donation of our used clothes and expired medicine to treat their malaria problem, though they are numerous in number, they would never agree together to move forward because of the conflicts that will be among them because of ethnicity and religion of Islam and Christianity because we continue to issue visa to permit our missionaries to plant in their mind, fake interpretation of Koran and the Bible, so that their mind will be mess up in a way that they will be thinking of heaven and not be able to reach one accord to free themselves from this our religious agenda which is meant to keep them from thinking about the development of their nation for ever, so that instead of building a nation for their next generations, they would become terrorist ready to die because Koran teaches they should commit suicide at 23. despite the fact that Imam in Mecca and Pope are more than 80 years old and still lives among us, and not in caves.

My Lady the Queen, one of them may be wise enough to know that the reason God put river Niger and river Benue in their land is for irrigation purpose to irrigate their farm, O.k. then, lets help them to use the river for Hydro-electric power station, and set it up in a way that it will never work for ever under NEPA management, so that all of them will be in darkness, But my lady the Queen, but if they become hungry and start using the river for irrigation purpose, OH my God, while are you talking about this river all the time?

O.K. we know what to do, let us curse them in the name of the river, since their tradition have over five thousands of years covenant with Satan on flowing rivers, all what we have to do now is placed a jinx and spell on all of them and name the land after the name of a river in order to perpetuate generational curse on their generation fore ver. So that as long as the river flows, they will never have solution to their political and economic problems and they will wait upon our direction and protection for ever, and by the time we give them their independence, if some of them become agitate to be free from our labor, we would have been successful to curse the people of the land to remain our slaves for ever because of the covenant we made unconsciously on their behalf by naming the land after a river. So that we would be able to govern the land spiritually despite the fact that they are already free politically.

My Lady the Queen, what name shall will give to this your farm and plantation whose people are numerous and powerful laborers, The spirit of my ancestor in this England has agreed to call the plantation after a river, and the name shall simply be Niger river area, which we can simply short to a name Nigeria.

But My lady the Queen, calling the plantation on the name of the river, did not sound sensible to this Parliament, because it sound as if there is no people living in the land, Yes, tell the parliament that the name is given after river for spiritual reason to enslave the people that lives around the river as nobody in the spirit realm by a covenant made on their through their names with the gods of their masters, they are but laborers forever.

A name that is after a river, is an interpretation in the spirit realm, or the flying angels of blessing that this place is just a river and no man lives in the surrounding area, and the river is more important than the people if at all there is a people living in the area, so to the spirit all we are concern about and respect is whatever we can get out of the farmland not minding whosoever lives in that plantation, so in the spiritual realm, it is just like a plantation of which nobody lives in the surrounding area, because if we want to give it a name that will not subject the people living in that plantation to oppression and labor for life, all we would do is name the land after the people, and simply says the People Republic of Niger-river area, (**The People Republic of Nigeria**)

For our own control mechanism, do not let us put people in the name, that will make them free, so the land can be bless with petroleum, bitumen, iron and steel, but the people living in the land will not be free and be bless forever, so if you include people, that means we already put the people as important in the spirit realm because such name would suggest that the land is for the people who are in the land that owns the land, but Nigeria means this is The Queen plantation in Niger river area and nobody in history owns it but the Queen.

Before you go Mr. Parliament, these people were already divided by the river Niger and river venue into 3 nations, for a God plan to feed all year round these people that lives in the land, so river Niger is river Niger at the north side of the country, but it joined together with another river to flow in unity to the Atlantic Ocean, which provided a secret of stability and strength for the land, so if these 3 nations remain as one, no nation in this planet would be able to stand against them, so let us allow the selection of their leadership in this our plantation on religion and ethnicity in other to prevent their unity for advancement through zoning formula, use them against them on religion, then use the over 300 ethnic languages to promote the issue of traditions and customs differences to separate the Obis. the Obis and the Emirs on ethnic difference, then we would conquer them forever, and whatever may be their natural resources they would never be able to manage it, without us in the future, so if at all we give them independent, 100 years later, without us there would not be anything that they can do for themselves without us, because of the division we put in place today through religious differences and ethnicity to separate them and the curse of naming the land after a river without signifying in the name that somebody lives in the land enough to be them in generational bondage as a people.

But My lady the Queen, what if some of them who are your body guards now, this body guards that have access to this information decided as your own trained Security Guards to free his own people?

O.K. Mr. Parliament, Have you not read Exodus 5: 10-23? put sanctions on the country, and use the media propaganda to create a conflict among them, so that from coup to coup they shall end up moving around this mountain forever, this names signify that no human beings lives in this land, it's just a plantation and oil field where the Queen laborers work with a pay of under $1 a day in 2010.

If those Ogonis, stubborn Niger Delta laborers cry foul. Deal with them with my son Mr. America who migrated from this palace few hundred years ago, and God has blessed him so much and he is now the world commissioner of police, he will take of any of them who may want to cause trouble, and try to free his own people.

I Emmanuel Oluwole Adetula, A Citizen of Nigeria by birth having considered the above spiritual allegory, hereby proposed a new name for this new nation in this revolution, that will notify the spiritual realms that human beings lives in this land, and that this land is no longer the plantation of the Queen, nor does it belong to Mr. America his son, and we the people who lives in this land are no longer the Queen laborers but this day hereby served the Queen a notice of resignation as his laborers from this day forth. she can keep his change. because he never pay us salary anyway, so we go free today to set up our own business under a new name registered by us as one of the pillar of the new world order, and we own all the 100 percent shares to this land, and the time for us to go has come, we are moving forward to cross the river with this new name we have carried for over 50 years. we as a people have move round this mountain for long, we determed to be free at last, let it be known. let it sound across to every principalities and power, and rulers of the darkness of this age, and tell the princes and princess of all land and the power that rules in every nations of this world. that I the prince of the Niger has proclaimed this day a new name for this land, and I hereby demand respect from all the princes and princesses of this planet, that my people will no longer serve any other kings and Queens, but will remain free, for it is better now for us to be a king in this our castle than rather be unrecognized chief in any kings palace as free people, Have not heard. has it not been told you, that it is written, He raised up the poor from the dust and the needy from the dunghill, and make him to sit among the princes and the princes of his own people, this is the day that God has made, Let us rise up, Fire up and let us go and possessed our destiny and become free at last with a new name that identified the people as the ownership of this land. By the authority and anointing of God that is upon my life to lead this revolution, I hereby revoked the certificate of occupancy of the Queen over this land with immediate effect, and this land no longer belongs to any river gods and goddesses but to all my people of Nigeria in the name of ALLAH and the in the name of one only Jehovah God as revealed by his son Jesus Christ. Amen—People let's do it, let the freedom reign. Let it rain.

We the people of this land will no longer be subject to the gods and goddess of the Queen of England, or his son Mr. America and from this day let there be a new a name, let their arise today the unity of the people across this land and let us go free with a new name as a United People of Nigeria in this our United States of Niger-area, and let the freedom rain. And let it rain. Let it be proclaim in every Cities, towns, villages and Hamlets, that today a freedom has be given by God to the sleeping giant of Africa, to rise up and take her rightful place in the new world order. Thank God we are free at last, free, free at last!

Making FEAR TO BECOME AFRAID

If Martin Luther King Jr., Muhammad Gandhi was here in our time, the security council's at the United nations would have agreed together and label them a Terrorists to stop them from leading their own people to the land of political and economic freedom, because the new tool in the current world order being use to stop developing nations or third world countries by the great grand children of the imperialist masters and the great grand uncles and nephews of the slave masters is to use Ibo, Yoruba and Hausa against themselves in their own country, that is why when good thing happens in Nigeria the western media will not report it, but would capitalized on Nigeria simple ethnicity problem or a case of an alleged 23 year old Nigerian terrorist boy for 3 months on their radio and television with their propaganda machinery in order to police Nigerian freedom and maintain a statue quo in Nigeria, by recruiting their own secret agents that will be in Nigeria to monitor the movement of Nigerian potential leaders with the plan to label them as terrorists, so that Nigeria will remain forever their plantation and oil fields to supply them timbers for their housing needs and oil and gas for their energy needs, but unfortunate for these arrogant masters, Nigeria has crossed over the red sea today.

I am not a Nigeria Moses, so you do not have to bother yourself to put me under a terrorist watch lists, and I am not John the Baptist either, though I eat Grasshopper, Akuta and Agbogboluju as an Owo man from Ondo state like John, please don't bother yourself to include me in no fly terrorist list, anyway that lists are for poor people who use commercial flight, not someone with his own private jet, check my name on your computer, you will see that in the last 12 years that I never travel by any commercial flight, or don't bother to arrest me because of this book. hoping that you can put me away and do abortion to this Nigeria pregnancy that is why I am naming the baby "Revolution" because you want her to give birth to break up of the country to many smaller nations you can control effectively, but no sir, it's too late for you, the Mama Niger is giving birth very soon, and very soon, there is nothing you can do to me that will stop her to deliver this baby Revolution, mine is to speak the word, and what I have spoken I have spoken, and through the world of this book and by the grace that God has given me to establish the foundation for this revolution, those that will build upon this foundation are the Nigerians between the age of 18-62, not these elderly people you are paying through your donation and grant for your so call fundamental human rights and good governance to rule Nigeria on your behalf and report back to you their supervisor, and any time they failed to do things you paid them to do, you use simple matter like a 23 year old boy terrorist to remind your sponsored Nigeria leaders to tight their belt on the poor people running out from Nigeria because their father are rich, selfish and self-centered, have many wives, and want all his boys to accept the status quo, and anyone of them who disagreed with the rich Alhajis greediness for money and power. will receive his wrath. make life so difficult for his own son with his powerful connection in the country and abroad and now go to US Embassy to disallow him to run away to other country, not because this rich fool love US, No, he is afraid of the boy, so he put pressure on this 23 year old boy until he decided to commit suicide, and the best way to commit suicide nowadays is to be a terrorist and die honorably, why should a 23 years old boy want to commit suicide by terrorism if the rich father is not an abusive father. someone should talk about these abusive Nigerian fathers who are selfish, arrogant polygamist. stole all the money in first bank.shared and enjoy the money with his numerous wives and concubines. now lost control of the management of his children, and now report his child who disagreed with capitalism with no human face for the welfare of its 70% of the country population, why do you think a boy of age 23 born by a rich man want to die, and kill 243 people together with himself, was it Osama Bin Laden teachings? No, the answer is that Obasanjo joined the Army at 21, returned back to Ota his home town at the age of 42 after he has served as Nigeria Head of State, Gowwon became Nigeria Head of Sate at 29, but Nigerians youth of today between the age of 21-30 are jobless despite the fact that they are attended the best university in the world, unlike Gowon and Obasanjo who went to military college to learn how to plan coup and rig elections. Major in coup planning and election rigging, minor in farming.

I submit to you that there are more than twenty million Nigerians between the ages of 20-60 who are university graduates in Nigeria today contemplating suicide because of the vagabond in power at Abuja, I have done my job by writing this book, there lied in wait for the launching day of this revolution, let those who is planning to stop it, receive this notice to rent out their mansion and prepare to go on exile, because when this is over, these young guys of over twenty million youths will disobey their fathers and carry out the words of this book, and your opposition using your media to ridicule this revolution on that days will not last more than 100 days, then there will arise a new dawn of new era in Nigeria, and my people shall be free from their arrogant greedy and selfish fathers who care less about the next generations, so mark my word, what I have written, I have written, these boys and girls will build upon this my foundation and you will see it. There is nothing anybody does to me that will stop this revolution; the freedom will rain very room.

Your game to Nigeria in 2010 is just for Nigerian government to allow you to build, expand, and equipped your nuclear power station in Nigeria to monitor the whole African continent, and since some elected leaders refused to allow your hundred percent management of such station in their own country by your own citizens, just like the Queen rule her Niger-area plantation by appointing British Citizen pre-independence, you now set up noise making at CNN all Nights as a legitimate reason to have your way in December 2009. using a 23 year old frustrated boy who should carry a revolution with his own father at home and him up with his concubines, You know why I love your game?, because Conflict management is one of the subject I studied in college, but watch this, go ahead, I love your idea, but remember that the coming Nigeria revolution will within first hundred days of the revolution take over any built nuclear facility in Nigeria by any foreign country, suspend production of oil in Niger delta for 100 days, and resume control of the Nuclear station by a force of power to generate electricity in villages and Urban cities for the 140 million people, despite the fact that the station remote control will be taken away that day by the builder. but remember these boys are jobless nuclear engineer, who have nothing to do with their brain than internet scam and terrorism, should knows how to operate Nuclear power station anyway, it's not me that will do it, because I am just a Pastor preaching this message from my bully pulpit, those boys are capable to put an end to importation of Generators to Nigeria to provide electricity to the rich, so you feel me now?, do we have an understanding here?, This revolution is not about me, I am not a terrorist, and have no plan for jihad as an anointed and licensed minister of God, so Let the Homeland security guards knows that I Tula owns no pistol or gun, and will not fire a shot to accomplish this revolution, my weapon is my fingers and my mouth, I use my fingers to write as I am doing here right now, and mouth to devoured the spoil, and when I start roaring you will know a lion is a lion, whether in the jungle of Africa or cage in Los Angeles Zoo right now, and I may not need to make a public speaking before the start of this revolution, and I do not need to be in Nigeria to start it, because I have spoken this world into the atmosphere, it has travel from Pacific Ocean from window frontage through the same canal where the boats transported African slaves to America, and my words now rules the Atlantic ocean, the day has come for the freedom of the black race, let their arise the people of Nigeria and free themselves from the tyranny of power, the time do it is now, since I don't want to dance myself lame now, until the main dance is yet to come, I will not answer your question in this interview, so no comment, read this book and all the rest of my books, and you will know that I am not a comedian, but a man set-up for this time to make fear to become afraid, so if you are afraid of me as being a dangerous man, that is normal, I am sorry, I can't help you from being afraid of me, anyway you never trust any Nigerian, you already made up your mind that all of us are scam artists and terrorist anyway, so what I can advise you to do is to see your doctor, or a counselor, for your psychiatric evaluation since you have a public health insurance, and make sure you take your medicine if you get mad because of my writings, because I will accomplish this assignment, because what God asked me to do is to write down what he revealed to me about the future of Nigeria. That is exactly what I did as a minister of God, with fear of no man, and so what I have written, I have written. Some Nigerian in Diaspora will come back home permanently, and this revolution will allow opposition of this people liberty and freedom to peacefully lease their mansions and go into exile until a seasons has passed over them and they come to realized and accepted that it is God that rules in the kingdom of man, he put one down and lift another one up for his plan and purpose in this planet, says the Lord.

I am an anointed and ordained minister, my job as a political pastor is to tell the world through my bully pulpit as a paper tiger, and my weapon is only my mouth and fingers, writing with my fingers and talking with my mouth is my weapon not violence, and what I have said will come to pass, because the millions of the youth to carry it out are trained mind, educated, major in mechanical, electrical, nuclear engineering from colleges and universities around the world, but have no job when they come back home, and have no visa like me to run away from Nigeria, where we use our nuclear engineer degree to wash toilet because you cannot employed a green card holder immigrant in a foreign nuclear facility, because he is an immigrant, but you love to run it with your own citizen in another man country under the monitor eyes of united Nigga—UN, these my children who are in Nigeria that have job in Nigeria work for about $200 salary per year, less than $1 a day, they are millions of them in Nigeria, they are awaiting for the manifestation of the sons of God, and by the anointing of God that is upon my life, here come the man Tula who have been authorized by God to lay the foundation to change their thinking and free them from being a religious victims of Islam as terrorists but rise up to build a new nation, rebuild their own country, and come no more to America or Europe as immigrants, and stop the idea of being a terrorist, use your militant power towards your own home country nation building, and deliver yourself from being a victims of Islamic false teaching of using violence against others to please God.

LETTER TO Nigerian TERRORISTS

I will lead this revolution with a combine intelligent equilibrium gathering together Nigerians in Diaspora and at home, these group of men and women between the age of 18-60 will draw the idea of a country with force of Arms and diplomacy that are conform to the rules and order of international laws, an idea that will defend the territorial integrity of this modern Nigeria, there will not be room for current Nigerian aristocrats or the Czarists in this revolution, we would sought to defend our people and advance our national interest while promoting universal values and treating the two pursuits as complementary.

The clash between Christianity and Islam, which characterizes our Country Nigeria, actually has its roots imbedded deeply into world history. Indeed, the development of these two religions has occurred largely side-by-side. With that development has come considerable friction and societal unrest. There are many similarities in both the impetus for the development of these religions as well as many similarities in their impact on Nigerians

Both Islam and Christianity have a phenomenal impact in Nigeria. One of the most obvious impacts is the advent of what many in Western society are beginning to view as a religious war. Acts as atrocious as the September 11, 2001 destruction of the World Trade Center and the subsequent attacks on the United States Pentagon itself have been attributed to Islam. So too have many other bombings and killings around the world. The attacks on Nigerians by Nigerians today, and Nigeria being trained by Al Queda today as a terrorist are just one more manifestation of the deeply rooted tensions, which exist between Christians and Muslims in Nigeria. These tensions are only going to continue to escalate as the growth of Islam continues to escalate in this country. The discovery of Oil in Muslim Countries, and with oil being the major export earning of Nigeria where

65-70% of Nigeria people claimed to be Moslem, and the moral failure of Nigerians Ibo and Yoruba who has embraced western culture has become a factor which continue to encourage the thriving of Islam Jihad in Nigeria, which now make terrorism attractive to those seeking a change in the way they view their relationship with their God as Moslem, because the teaching of Islam offers enough variety from the mainstream traditional and culture of the Yoruba and the Ibo cultural and their traditional religion dated back to over 5000 years. The reasons Islam spread so quickly in Nigeria are not only attributable to society's joint needs for familiarity and variation, however. Its spread is attributable too much deeper aspects of societal need as well. It made its initial advent at a time when many of the world's cultures were ready for a dramatic change in the way they viewed their world and their interaction in that world. These cultures were willing to fight for that change, and Nigerian Imams used that opportunity of "Conquering armies and migrating tribes that swept out of Arabia, to spread Islam with the sword as much as with persuasion into the northern part of Nigeria, therefore this revolution task to keep Yoruba, Ibo, and Hausa nations as ONE NIGERIA, but we can only achieve this objective only by the adoption of Nigeria as a SECULAR STATE.

The historical impact of the friction between Christianity and Islam has recently been brought to our consciousness by the problems we are dealing with today. The clash, which has existed, between Islam and Christianity however, has resulted in many misperceptions and misunderstandings as to exactly what each of these cultures entail. In order to overcome these misperceptions and misunderstandings this revolution has decided to adopt a secular state, this is only way we can overcome one of the most serious threats to Nigeria stability that we are facing in Nigeria right now.

If you are a trained terrorist and you are a Citizen of Nigeria, do not kill yourself in the process of Jihad warfare against the Americans, I have a better life for you to do back at home, that will benefits the lives of about 140 million Nigerians, instead of using your talent, gifts, educational college degrees, training and skills, or bombs making skills acquired at al-queda camp to destroy Americans and Israel, come back home and join this revolution, because this revolution is set to free and build your own country and make it as powerful as America and Israel, so together as Nigerians we can do this, you have a better rewarding thing to do through this revolution as Nigerian better than the order given you by Osama Bin Laden to go and kill the infidels, come on now my brothers, let us use our skill together back home to support this revolution as brothers and sisters, as Moslem and Christians, and let our people be set free from the imperialist agenda of the east and the west, and let us change the game from game 8 to game 9, through our industry and human resources as a people, because life is a stage, you have been educated and trained as a game player, come home and let us play and work together on the stage of life to rebuild the falling walls of Nigeria, if you use your skills in a positive way to build a new Nigeria, that idea and pursuit will be more rewarding to you when you get to heaven, than killing yourself according to the tenets of the Koran as taught by your Imam, come on home, and together we can build Nigeria through this revolution and make it a super power in the comity of nations, I need you, your parents need you, your brother and sisters at home need you, we will miss you, if you die now trying to kill other people with bombs, I understand your frustration and concern as Moslem, I was a victim of religion myself, listening to preachers and prophets who interpreted the bible to me. an interpretation that deceived me for 13 years, before I went to study religion myself, I got my some of my degrees through university online studies. not because I want to work for a corporation or become a staff member of any private or government institutions, but to be informed about religion having been born in all my life, and to know how religion does cross the road with my psychology and my poverty dynastic as a black man, in my study of religion, sociology, negotiation and conflict management, I have come to realized that some of us will be rewarded in heaven only for the good we did for others when we get back to heaven, not the blood we shed trying to be soldiers and police for God and force any infidel to join our religion or get kill, it is now clear to me that you can win an infidel with love to your side than by force of Arms, because God hate violence, particularly when you do it as pre-empt strike against other nation, and not doing it just to defend someone who has come to your own fatherland to take your land from you, and the service that God required from all Nigerians between the age of 18-60 years old now is to be part of this revolution and build Nigeria nation into a super power like America. That was why God put you through all what you now understood as your own experience and capability, do not loose your life in the name of Jihad, the new assignment of Jihad, that God has for you now as a Nigeria, is to build your father's homeland and help the poor and the needy to get a better reward than shedding other people blood and in the process hurt or kill yourself?.

This reason God allow you to be trained as fighter is to come back to Nigeria and join Nigeria National Guard or member of Nigeria Revolution

Intelligent Agency, to protect your own country against foreign aggression, not to go and blow up airplane and kill American in America, or be planning to wipe out Israel from the map, Israel is a nation that grow rice in the desert to feed his own people, and their desert land is just as the desert land of the northern part of Nigeria who import rice to feed its own people, don't you think of it for a moment that we need a partnership with irrigation technology of Israel to make the northern part of Nigeria the food basket of Africa instead of importing rice to Nigeria in 2010, we have own problem at home, while setting yourself on fire with bomb making devices that may end up killing with yourself and may be with five other people?. You are too bless and talented to get yourself in that kind of a thing, but here in Nigeria your skill can help 5 million out of poverty, if you agree with me today to use your skill and talent to work for a better life for your brothers and sisters and family members here at home, I know from my own study of Koran and the bible and by God revelation to me as regards this revolutions that every Nigerian born between 1950-1990 hold the responsibilities to rebuild Nigeria, and that not one of us is sent to this planet by God to busy himself with a plan to kill American wherever they are, God want you to help your own people and family in poverty in Nigeria, your fight now should be against those who will come to Nigeria to stop us from accomplishing our goal for this revolution, do not go to them to strike them. come home; let's build this fallen wall together with your skill, while some will be building this our father's wall. you will carry the sword to defend the builders as a member of the national guard to defend any internal and external forces that want to stop our freedom, we would not fight anyone, but whosoever come here to stop this work will wake you up the sleeping tiger, then you will fight to defend your land, when I tell you to fight as Chairman of this revolution, don't you like that?.

Current Nigerian soldiers and police force working under this present leadership in Nigeria that is going to stop this revolution has not been born, that is why God trained you in Al Queada camp to defend this freedom in your homeland, let us put the pieces together, there and there and let my people unite, and let it be known to all the youth of this land that our youth no longer need any visa to destroy infidels anywhere to find them according to the Imams interpretation of the Koran, your assignment is to live a better life as a member of this revolution Nigerian Armed guard, Come back and let us build our fatherland and motherland, let the former plantation of the Queen be build by the remnants of her laborers, and let the laborers take over the 100% shares of the Niger-area land. and revoke the certificate of occupancy of the Queen, and let the freedom reign, you are too blessed my brothers to allow yourself to be living in cave.

You are not born as cave man in Afghanistan, Yemen, or somewhere out there in mountain valley, you are the man for this hour, come home, don't fear, your parents are ready to welcome you back home if you make the right choice today to change your mindset and be a good boy again, when your father's house is vacant at home while should choose to be hiding in the bush?. Come home son and there await you like a prodigal son, a good welcome to be part of the builders of our heritage, and let us leave a legacy behind in our own land, a legacy that will endure into eternity.

Imagine you have the opportunity to defend Nigeria territorial integrity as one of its national guard while you are being paid as a police officer or naval officer or air force soldier, using your skill in a profession for the right job in Nigeria, living a better happy successful and enjoyable life with your own house, your own car, 24/7 electricity in your home, portable drinking water, access to good health care services, that is coming to modern Nigeria nation through this revolution, where you will enjoy your life with your own wife and children, and be a defender of Nigerians freedom and its dream of a civil society rather to be hiding yourself in the caves. You feel me now, can we have understanding here.

All statistic about religion of Christianity and Islam in Nigeria are false, the truth of Nigerians religion are 32% Muslim, 15% Christians, and 55 % Satanism. The Ibo and Yoruba are nations with over 5000 years history in the mythology of Satanism, occultism and demonism, because every Yoruba or Ibo child is born into an ancestral burdens, foundational contamination with evil rituals dated back to seven generations, satanic family inheritance, ancestral yokes and burdens, unprofitable spiritual family heritage control mechanism, these issues is in the blood of every black man wherever they go, and these also affects all the black slaves that was brought to America from Africa, the reason African chiefs sold some slaves to Americans and British slave masters was to free their prison. just like in Los Angeles now trying to free their prison yards because they are broke and have not enough budget to take care of the people in jails, imagine if somebody come from Canada today and said he need slaves, Obama the President of America will quickly direct his commander to sell the terrorist in Quintana to them, that is why you have now African American, therefore any black man anywhere in the world is affected negatively in the spiritual realm not by an act of his character. so a black man problem is not a social problem, it is a spiritual problem. Not about him, it is about his age—long spiritual foundation, that is why for a black man to be free he or she must take serious his or her spiritual life, since we Nigerians understand that fact, that is why we pray too much and spend all days in the church, not like these white guys or the Jews or the Arabs, because Koran is Arabs forefathers history, Bible is the forefathers history of the Jews, but the Negro book was destroyed and burnt by these Nigga, and so you now have the right to mess up our lives with your books, Paul did not write any letter to Ibo man or Yoruba man, or may be King James of England removed it from the Church bible, so we have our problems, and you have use religion of books to enslave us as slaves for long, and now you are using it to mess up the life of our children still in 2010, enough is enough for this East and west imperialist agenda against the black race, come home my brothers. let the freedom reign. We have job to do, give them back their bombs and let us move our nation into freedom.

For over seven years in America I have been working with the homeless population, through my non-profit organization "CCN House Community Development Agency", and 60% of my clients are African American Blacks, and I challenge American government to eradicate welfares from the state today, this spiritual truth will be revealed to them that, an average black man or woman in America will lives under a dollar a day just like a Nigerian in Nigeria, so the difference between the blacks in Africa and the African America blacks in America is America **compassionate capitalism** that allows welfare of the people in the management of its capitalist economy and that is why my administration in this revolution in Nigeria will adopt in his totality the America idea of welfare to the poor, a program that I have witnessed and participated in for this past seven years in America, this is one of the cornerstone of this revolution to take care of all the 70% of Nigeria population that lives today under $1 a day. And this idea is not negotiable with any arrogant far right in Nigeria. Any Nigeria capitalist or selfish millionaire who think he can stop this revolution from achieving welfare for the people of Nigeria through this revolution, should start advertising his or her mansion for lease and prepare to go peacefully to exile, before the day. For the time for my people to go is now, let the freedom reign, and let it rain.

Come back home baby and let the freedom rain, I love you my brothers, come on home and let us make a new nation, for our generation was not born to destroy and kill other nationality or to hate the Israel, Koran and Bible are both a religion of peace and love, and compassionate to ones brothers and sisters, because we all serve one God, so our purpose should be in this age to re-build Nigeria into a new nation where freedom and liberty will rain, so that generations after you will have your name honorably display on their streets as a man who is a part of the greatest generations that ever live in Nigeria, and not as terrorist from Nigeria.

Which one do you want to choose today? because laid before you today is life or death, choose to live in cave as Jihad fighter ready to die in the process of want to kill American or the Israel people (or) to live in a new nation of Nigeria under one God, one people and one destiny where you will be free to practice your religion of Islam in peace with your fellow Christian brothers and sisters, and when you die and get to heaven, you will be rewarded as a man that help his own people out of suffering, poverty and oppression, How about that?. Come on home brother, if you choose life and let us roll and re-build Nigeria through this revolution and let my people be free, and let the freedom reign.

What do I have to fear? What shall separate me from this revolution shall fear of death, prison, persecution, and sanctions, local oppositions of the ignorant and self centered Nigerians there in Nigeria who will condemn this book? Or sword of its corrupt police? For I reckon that the suffering of my people this present time are not worthy to be compared with the glory which shall be revealed in us through this revolution. For I am persuaded, that neither death, nor principalities, no super powers, nor things present, nor things to come, nor any creature shall be able to separate us from this revolution, Nay, the years I have been in this planet is far more than the one I have left to remain here, An average Nigeria man life span is 50-70 years old, and if he has a good health like me, may be 80, how much do I have left to live? That I will refuse God assignment and purpose for my life? For I know that when I shall leave this body, I know where my soul and spirit is going, it is appointed unto a man to die once, after this come judgment, and the judgment is this, light come to the world, but man loves darkness rather than light because their deed are evil, and they are judged because they refused the light, the life of a man is like a vapor, it appears in the morning and in the evening it's no more, a man born of woman is but for short period of time in this planet and his days is full of sorrows, for as many as are led by the spirit of God, they are the children of God, I am led by the spirit of God to do this. I have become obedient to the voice of heaven, therefore one thing I hope to live for in the rest of my days on this planet is to work unashamed towards the believe of this revolution and left this country and this planet to become a better and save place. so that generation after me will live in peace happiness and prosperity, having established a legacy of freedom and liberty that will stand the test of time and endure in love unity and nationalism and the rule of law and order for all the people of Nigeria. Let the freedom reign.

If you are married to a Nigeria Christian woman, she will still settled a disagreement with you by consulting a prophet to help her with rituals, because the government do not have a system to address domestic violence, youth counseling, children custody, and restraining order to prevent violence, so the society forced you to click to a spouse when he is abusing you, and the police are not trained in the policy of domestic violence crisis management.

Nigeria has no child welfare program, the justice system are primitive in their ways of handling family related cases, so 90% of Nigeria Christians do not settle family problems by calling the police or going to court, but goes straight to prophets, or consult their mother who have address list of witchdoctors to defend her and fight for her through many white garment churches working in spiritual partnership with Moslem Alfas, these witchdoctors work in consultation with herbalists, to settle score with a close family members. So we Nigerians live our life among wicked family members seeing the brother or sister next room as a terrorist, so while do I have to fear a terrorist who is my brother to back come home? for over 40 years God has made me to survive all my family terrorists, and I even stay in same room right away from the sixth month we met, She try to kill me, and I still continue to sleep with her in same bed for 13 years, and I am still here, and two of my reward for having an alignment with her are now university college graduates at 23 and 22 years of age, so I have no republican fear of terrorists, and that does not mean I am a democrat. I will work with anybody that I need to work it, in order to leave a better life for Nigerian youths who have been frustrated by past Nigerian leadership bounce checks. Come, I say come, come home brothers and let us work together, it's them who are afraid of you, everyday they seek to kill me from the very day that I lost my mother as a baby boy in 1964, my own family terrorist, and I am still here, who care about terrorists, I will put all of you to work in the new social order, and you will ever forget that other nations exist beside Nigeria, because together we can use our human and natural resources to transform Nigeria and match it one-on one with these developed nations. Let the freedom rain, and let my people go.

If I have done this as a result of my own ambition you shall stop it, and even self stopping me TULA will not result into stopping this revolution, but if this revolution is in God plan for his people, you will be put to shame and the name of your family will be wipe out from the leadership of mankind to the seven generations for working against this God plan. This revolution is set for the rising and falling of many. If God be for us who shall be against us? Anyone who tries to stop this Nigeria revolution will begin it with the death of his first-born, and quit the idea with his last born, says the Lord! For it is written torch not my anointed and do my prophet no harm. For whom he did foreknow, he did predestinate, and he also has been called, he will justified him, and then he shall be glorified. What I have written, I have written, and all my words of this book shall come to pass in the history of man, let the freedom reign.

AFRICA IS A gun, Nigeria IS THE Trigger

Nigerians have wondered in this desert since October 1960, we are now at the bank of Jordan, there will now arise from sokoto to calabar the great grand children of the oppressed of my people who will rise up to free themselves from the great grand children of the imperialist masters, that day the heart of the children will go against their parents religion, culture and tradition, for the current pregnancy of conflict of Mama Niger will not brake Niger-area into pieces under my watch, but shall result into a currency of a revolution that will unite the people from the established mafia and there will arise a new name, a new people of a new culture, one destiny. one people, one nation under one God where traditional rulers, the military, religion and the western powers are completely separated from the control of the politicians running the state, from that day power shall rest with the people by the people to serve the people, that day freedom will rain and my people will be free. And we shall be free at last, and this revolution is not negotiable because I will not sit at any table with the arrogant far right of this planet to negotiate away this opportunity to free my people from you sir. Let my people go and let the freedom rain.

Looking at the geographical map of Africa, if you pick it up and turn it horizontally, it looks like a short pistol/gun. Then I saw a man out of my brethren, does he forgot to take his medicine? Is he crazy? Or is he sick, maybe he did not have public health Insurance, because there is no public option for the poor like him? I see this man rise up among my people. He picked up Africa and turns the gun to the Atlantic Ocean, in his hand Nigeria looks to me like the trigger of the gun, he pulls the trigger. and there appeared evaporation from Africa a thick form of darkness, the darkness that came out of Africa flows into the Atlantic ocean. then

I saw a great light that lighten the whole continent of Africa just by the act of the pulling Nigeria as the trigger of Africa, then I see that lights and freedom of Africa is hidden by God from the foundation of the world upon the revolution that is about to happen in Nigeria. No wonder the whites enslaved South Africa for a long time and now are using western media to stop Nigerians breakthrough, because what is happening in South Africa right now is the cleaning of the outlet of this gun. but when shall Nigerians pull this trigger? The darkness in Africa is waiting for the honest, sincere leadership of Nigeria by other African nations, therefore the time has come for Nigeria to act and pull itself as the trigger of Africa and let the darkness comes out from the hole prepared as South Africa into the Atlantic Ocean, or let the great grand children of the Slave Masters and the great grand Uncles and Nephews of the Imperialists Media who thinks no nation can survive their sanctions mentality with their media propaganda weapons try to stop this revolution. But I see condemnation of the revolution everywhere, and sponsorship of other Nigerians to work in the spirit of Sambalat and Tobiah to stop this revolution, despite America antagonism as self appointed world police officer, and the super power ritual to make the revolution feel isolated, the revolution care less about the jaw-jaw of United Nations, the conference table failed to stop Chairman Tula because every super power that stand before this revolution, does not stand for more than 100 days, and thereafter I see a dawn of new era of peace of nationalism with one accord, one people, one nation under one God of the United People of Nigeria. Let the freedom rain.

I will do a great thing in Nigeria says the Lord, the ear that hearth it shall tingle; Niger will be shaken for everything that need to be shaken shall be shaken when I shall start. Let mi sing it to you in Yoruba language) (*Emi yio se nkan ribi ribi ni ilu Nigeria, eti to ba gbo a gho yaya, Niger a mi titi, Oro ti mo ko fun yin ase o, ase o, ti mo ba bere, ase ohooo.*) For I have heard the groaning of my people Nigerians, their cry of oppression has come up to me in their churches and Mosques, I have come down to deliver them, I have raise my son for these days, and it shall come to pass that I will rebuke Obas, Obis, Emirs, or traditional rulers or religious leaders that stands in the way of this revolution, for such shall spend the rest of their days in exile while his palace will be converted to a playing ground by the local government for the children recreation and playing ground in the community says the Lord!. What I have written, I have written. In sha-Allah.

The impact of the current conflict in Nigeria and mass unemployment, lack of purpose and direction for her educated youths and the insults we in Diaspora takes every day in Pharaoh plantation where we cut grass with our green grass cutting permit and green, yellow, red and blue card, which gave us the opportunity to remove our own family to live with us in Diaspora, and the opportunity to send money back home to our own family left there in Nigeria has removed us just like the 10% political leadership. we no longer feel the pain of the poor as the Emirs, Pastors. Obis. Obas, Chiefs and the get rich quick Internet fraud scammers, and the politicians who drives around the bad roads in their imported cars, surrounded by security thugs, blowing siren as a sign of immunity against the problem of 90 % of the people who lives under $1 a day.

This scenario of conflict among Nigerian people has reached the boiling point that its ability to affect all geographical areas would be the key determinant to bury once and for all the power and influence of the slave masters who continue to use religion and ethnic difference to divide and rule my people, the sign of time, and the season for this revolution is now written on the wall, let those who are wise see it, and let the fools fall for lack of knowledge of its coming, for this revolution will occurred soon on a national scale to give birth to a new nation based on nationalism that will wipe out ethnicity, there will arise from its past, a new day where Hausa will be brothers of an Ibo man, and Yoruba will embrace Fulani girl as a Sister, the wall erected as barrier by the religion of Islam and Christianity will be pull down, and traditional rulers dictates to political leadership will become history, and the will of the people will reign in the land.

The power of the western media propaganda will become a laughing stock in the committee of United Nations, because Nigeria revolution will rise on the fasted lane of information technology and match power to power in the media propaganda warfare with the west, making fear to become afraid.

Because propaganda is the greatest form of warfare in the 21st century, this coming Nigeria revolution understand this truth and we will use it match to match, one-on-one and Nigeria revolution refused to play anymore the role of a sleeping giant of Africa in the coming new world order that is about to emerge under one global currency. Our political position remains alliance with only those who supports this revolution and is will defiant with no apology to those who opposed this movement of the people, no more bounced checks, all we want is let my people go, and let the freedom and liberty reign.

THE Ideology OF THIS Revolution

This revolution will not go to the far left of communism because some Nigerians are naturally lazy, and want other family member to go to work and provide for their needs while they remains as do nothing people, and this revolution will not allow itself to introduce socialism in the governance of the state either, because of the custom, tradition, and the ethnic history of its people and the religion of Islam and Christianity that represented the faith of the people of Nigeria, we have taken the position of not evolving into Socialism or communism because a nation is not a natural phenomenon, rather it is an artifact, a product of happenstance, human ingenuity, with all the resulting possibilities for successful trial and error, because a revolution. when you are at it is horrible and dull, it is when you achieved the goal that all people will see your idea as divine, and would then want to participate in it as their own destiny.

I am not advocating here or enticing Nigerian people to move to Socialism or Communism because the crime which Socrates was condemned—was for his refusal to accept the religion of the state in conformity with the spirits of religion that the majority of his people believe as a way to reach their gods, but I promised the world that I will not laid the foundation of this new nation in the gloomy age of ignorance and current religious superstition of Islam or Christianity, like we see presently today in 2010 Nigeria, I have studied this 2 religions and their occidental history, and will not allow these two religion to interwoven themselves in the management of the state, but this revolution will eventually replace monarchies, not through force of arms, but through democracy itself, for this revolution shall be based not on blood but the purity of idea.

After its first year in power, once this revolution cleansed the shameful past and stain corruption of Nigeria past leadership, the path will be lay open to Africa continent hegemony, and Nigeria control of African leadership will open way to the influence of a black man in the global market.

My personal objective in this revolution is to vindicate the principle of peace, prosperity, freedom and liberty of my people, and to render justice in the life of this nation as against the current selfish and autocratic leadership set up to make as an alien about 70% of Nigerians in country of their birth, with lack of equal distribution of opportunities. If I am able to do this I would see myself has having been successful to make this nation itself free at last.

From this time henceforth, I issue a decree that the people of Nigeria may now be dominated and governed only by their own consent through the ballot box through free and fair election and self determination, any election rigging from today will be revolutionary rejected by the people, from the local level to the presidency, the current imposed zoning system is hereby abolished, this principle now becomes an imperative principle of action which should begin now in every villages, towns, cities and hamlets, no one should wait for me, let the revolution begins now today according to my word, of which statesmen will henceforth ignore at their peril, any statesman who ignore my word in this book from today does so at his or her own risk.

I call on all men and women, boys and girls to fire-up, be ready to go and defend your own freedom from the greediness of our fathers, and build for yourself a better future, don't wait for me because I am free and happy in United States and I am still here as a legal permanent resident, so if you need me, you know where to get me, let the freedom rain, and let it rain.

If the homeland security guard too want me they know where to get me, Abraham Lincoln and Hitler are reminders of the crucial role that individuals have played in determining the fate of nations, therefore Chairman Tula is not ashamed to lunch this revolution, that will make Nigeria as a nation to rise into a prominent global super-state, the time is against me now to postponed this assignment because of the pregnancy for conflict in Nigeria, and the suffering of my people whose ambition is to get a visa and become an immigrant in another countries, the time for Nigeria revolution is now, let the freedom rain. The Lord is my light and my salvation, whom shall I fear anyway? Let the freedom rain.

The beginning of this revolution in Nigeria is not an end in itself; it is only a stage on our way to the organized nation of tomorrow, this start is to bail us out from the prison camp of the conquerors, since the culture and tradition of our people are woven around the facts that no Nigerian is respected or valued if he or she is poor, a culture, tradition and believes that value its citizens on the type of clothes, shoes, type of cars you drive, the kind of house you live, the amount of money you have in your pocket and in your bank account. your family background, or is your parents rich or poor? This materialism concept that have eaten deep to the mindset of the people for over 50 years has grown to become Nigeria acceptable norms of life, and since such way of thinking is woven in capitalism, it cannot be removed in a day, people of Nigeria do not valued themselves on character, attitude, disposition, or heroism, that is why the internet scammers continues to operate because the society do not required from them where and how they got their money from?. The ones in Diaspora committed fraud and come back home to display the ill-gotten wealth, he is embraced because he has money, and nobody care what does he did in London or in US to get all these dollars and pound sterling?

Majority of people are money conscious, marriages are based not only on love but how much money you got to give the bride and your in-law, tradition demand you paid for getting a wife, which they called in our tradition as OWO-ORI, the bride price, I am still single today because I was a revolutionary against the tradition or may I did not have money to pay to get one wife, so if you have money, you can get many women, or someone with more money can your wife from you as the highest bidder supported by your wife family when you travel out of town because they gave out their daughter in marriage based on money received from the rich man, having considered all this with my experience in Nigeria and here with Nigerians in United Sates, and the African American community. I submit therefore that we shall be building this new nation on error of history if we embrace communism or total socialism, as a black man, because some ethnic groups contributed nothing to the plate but want everything for themselves. some loves to dance all day, drinks, party, sex, produce children with many concubines and does nothing to contribute to the economy, but lives in congested urban centers looking to Abuja to rain bread from heaven.

The only thing some Nigerians take serious is going to church and mosque, and some are converted Christians, but they remain a Moslem because it allows them to keep four wives, some claimed to be born again Christians, but because of money they goes to witch doctors for help, so if you do not have money or material procession as a Nigerian, it becomes a stigma and people look at you that your life is worthless and it does not matter how many university degrees you have, poverty is perceived as things caused by you, or your own destiny, or your family curse and generational spells, therefore people disassociated themselves from you just like they treated people with HIV/AIDS, so to an average Nigerian it is not about your good character but how much money you got? To them poverty is a dreaded blood disease classified in the category of leprous, and HIV/AIDS, and you are alone by yourself if you are poor, and because the religion of Islam see your disease of poverty as your own problem and destiny placed upon you by Allah, you lives your life in anger with yourself and the state who refused to bail you out, and when come election year, the rich will give the poor $2 to get their vote, same reason same candidates will direct the affairs of the state for another four years, because of mass poverty ; Nigeria poor make bad choices in other to survive on daily basis, having considered the mindset of my people in Africa and here in United States, and having work with the homeless and the poor in Los Angeles the homeless capital of America with 51% of my clients the homeless and poor people as blacks, I will suggest that this revolution should start with the practice of liberal and compassionate capitalism with welfare programs for the needy and the poor, this I know will work for now to play a just society for all. So when I handed over the leadership of this revolution to the next generation of leadership, they could by them from my experiment decide the type of ideology suited for the new nation.

This revolution will create a national welfare programs agenda for all Nigerians to give all the poor free access to health care services, free education, food programs welfare system and housing for all, create employment and unemployment monthly cash allowance to the jobless graduates, and the state will support with grants, and partnership with civil society institutions anywhere in the world who has programs and projects to eradicate disease, poverty and illiteracy from the land, using all power of the state to free our people from poverty, and create a just society for all Nigerians, as contains in the reasons for this revolution as you read further in this book and as will be further detail in this revolution 2011 manifesto.

TEN REASONS WHY I ACCEPTED
THE leadership OF THIS
Revolution

The spiritual allegory of this revolution, and my letter to Olusegun Obasanjo

Chairman Tula

REASONS ONE FOR THIS Revolution

Nigeria is more like a region, a single country, a dominant in west Africa, a leader in Ecowas and NEPAD, Nigeria ranks 152 out of 175 countries on the UNDP human development index despite its position as the third largest oil exporter to the America market and its share on average is seemingly about 30% sometime of oil exported to us here in California.

Nigeria has the largest Muslim population in Africa, the sixth largest Muslim population in the world, out of about 140 million population, between 65-70-million claimed they are Moslem, therefore political parties always win election on religious affiliations, between Islamic believes and Christians believe, there is no way a democratic election can be established in Nigeria through the ballot box with no regard to Islamic faith of a presidential candidates at the federal level, and aspiration to leadership that did not separate Islam and Christianity from governance still in 2010 will not be possible to allow good leadership in Nigeria for the next 50 years, this is how religion has crippled Nigeria progress for the past 50 years of its independence, and I am not going to leave this planet and left my children in such a country. and I am not going to move my children from Nigeria with my legal residency in America because of bad leadership in Nigeria. and left 70 million Nigerians there like all of us in Diaspora are doing. when we make it as immigrants in other nations forget about them and let Nigeria continue to go down the drain because of religious leaders? I study religion, nobody can bull-sheet me about the game of religion in occidental history, therefore this revolution will completely separate religion from the state, and dump in the Atlantic ocean the current constitutional provisions that elevate religion above the freedom and progress of Nigerian people.

The new revolution constitution for the coming modern Nigeria, would contains a permanent clause that will completely separate religion of Islam and Christianity from the affairs of state, in the current scenario the constitution presented to us a problem which now make election to the presidency on the platform of you either be a Muslim to win about 70% of the population or choose a Muslim as your vice president, which has never profited us in the last 50 years, or gave Nigeria the right leadership that it deserved, this new revolution constitution is not negotiable, you cannot put a new wine in an old bottle, a new wine deserved a new bottle, there will be no provision of sharia or cannon law in the new constitution. this is not an Islamic State, and neither Bishop Vatican state to practice Cannon laws, because the new constitution is not going to be drafted anyway by any Nigeria above the age of 62. some will give some and some will give all, and at the end of the day, my people shall be free.

Imam is enjoying in Mecca, Pope for enjoyment in the vertican, my people in Nigeria in 2010 are still having annual per capita income of $300 as compare with $1,000 in 1970, In 1970s $1 is equal to one Nigeria money, now $1 is exchange for 140 Nigeria naira, that is how serious this vagabond in power at Abuja got Nigeria down to the bottomless ocean of life, 140 miles below the sea level, who will go with me to pull it out, not this pot belly politicians in Abuja, whose stomach is filled up with pounded yam and fufu, scattered teeth because of bush meat bones, all of them above the age of 62 needed to go on vacation to take care of their big pot belly stomach, and let those who are not sick do the job, this revolution shall be led by women and the young jobless Nigeria college and university graduates because they cannot continue to watch their fathers throwing away their future in their own eyes. making their life miserable because of religion of Islam and Christianity which they use to make victims of poverty by 70% of population, just like they sold into slavery some of the children to America some 400 years ago, leaders that lives in a way of not bothering about the next generations is over in Nigeria, that is why this revolution is not negotiable with American presidential system constitution. thank you America, we hereby return to you, your constitution that our parents borrowed from your library, it does not work for us, since we are not member of your sponsored agent in government. you have no say in this revolution, we would have a new constitution of a secular state, and religion will become a private matter between man and his God.

There will no longer be appointment or election into political office or civil service employment based on religion, but on character, attitude, disposition, competency and experience required to do the job to benefits our people. No application form will ask applicants about his or her religion or state of origin in appointment to any federal institutional or appointment to political office any longer in Nigeria.

Thanks you Pope, thank you Imam. Thank you Guru Maharajah if you are still at Ibadan and thank you Orunmila baba Ifa. This revolution is set up to break all satanic manipulations aimed at changing Nigeria destiny in the comity of nations, therefore we reject in its totality every evil collective unity organized in Saudi Arabia and in America against this revolution, and we shall loose our people from all power of the occult, witchcraft and familiar spirit, that has taken over the affairs of governance in Nigeria through evil curses, chains, spells, jinxes, witchcraft and sorcery control operating under the disguise of religious provision in the current Nigeria constitution and now. from this day we hereby as a people established in the realm of the spirit a new name, a new people, a new nation with one people, one nation under one true God that will release its blessing on all Nigerians everywhere, if we sincerely practice our faith in him with no violence. and no act of terrorism against other Nigerians or other nations of the world, and those with Pharaoh spirit that says my people with not go, let him start the opposition to this revolution by the death of his first born, and quit pursuing us to stop it at the death of his last born. Amen.

REASON TWO FOR THIS Revolution

The economy remains stagnant at a rate of about 4%, despite the current administration under Yar` Adua claim of renewal commitment to fight corruption, supporting services delivery and revitalizing of the economy, the efforts of this present administration is not yet felt because of decades of economic mismanagement, micro economic instability, political repression and institutionalized corruption undermined social and economic development, which now continue to fuel dramatic increases in poverty, the estimated $800 billion generated from oil over the past years did nothing in the hands of past leadership to improved the well-being of the mass of Nigerians with over 70% lives under $1 a day, while only about 10% share the wealth at the top, 10% survives in Diaspora, 10% work for the government under $300 a year salary, these 30% stockpiled the wealth in their big missions and real estate with no plan of investing the stolen money into the economy to give jobs to those who are trained in colleges or has completed apprentice training to work and earn a living, now they encourage the growth of churches and Islam to keep the poor people busy at the churches and mosques praying for Jesus to come back or the seven Imam to come and deliver them from only 10% of the population who are ready to use local police and the army to terrorized them from demanding their freedom, our boys now are traveling for cave training with the mentality of best way to live and die is to become a terrorist? Put your hope in heaven, then go drink, dance, party and go church or mosque, pray five times a day, when you die, you will be welcome by God in heaven, and the best way to have a high position and better mansion in heaven like Aso Rock is tight yourself to a bomb, blow-up the plane, kill 273 American people, the youth who are very intelligent and schooled

44

in the affairs of religion to a point that they have lost their reason power, therefore has failed in their civil duty to lead a resistance to bad leadership and mismanaging of resources by the government.

In 1980, 27.2 percent of Nigeria population or 18 million people, were classified as poor, this rate surged to 66 percent under the military ruler ship in 1996 survey and the total number of the poor now is nearly quadrupled to 70 percent in 2010, estimate put the poverty rate today to getting close to 75 percent or about 90 million people, perhaps, 50% of these people are the "core" poor, that is about 40% of Nigerians in 2010 are so impoverished that they cannot meet their basic food needs unless they have a family member like me in United states or in other developed nations washing toilets to send money to them to meet their food and clothing expenses, and money for beer to drink, cigar to smoke, then use part of it as tithes and offerings for the pastors, dance in church, and go and sleep or use my money from America to get another one more wife.

This scenario is stunting for young Nigerian children, a measure of chronic nutrition deprivation and food insecurity stand at 42 percent and food security in 2010 stands at 42 percent, which means 58 % of Nigerians living in Nigeria today does not have in their home what they would eat tomorrow, and despite this scenario, the present leaders at Abuja, both the executive and the legislatures have no solution to this problem, and all of them go to either church or mosque, and operate sharia laws on the poor people who have nothing to eat that cassava, the rural dwellers are moving from their agricultural base and profession to the urban area to feed themselves and their families. moving from villages where they are suppose to farm to feed themselves. which are complex with rapid growth of urbanization of towns with no drainage system and difficulties of service delivery in an environment pregnant with conflict that is about to explode with confrontation of Islamic and Christian religion with empty stomach which are sponsored by the east and western agenda to break this country into pieces, and all this is done now under the watchful eyes of these empty headed leaders who lack access to information about the coming world order, that the only legitimate power of Nigeria is its size and population. and if Nigeria does not remain one, and the Ibo, Hausa and Yoruba did not stick together in the spirit of nationalism, their place and resources will be taken over in the new world order and the coming one world government, so the agenda is break them to make them powerless, use religion and love of ethnicity to divide them, take what they have, and use them as modern slaves. and let the Niger-area becomes again our plantation, and oil and gas fields, while the indigene of the Niger area will once again be conquered as our slaves in the new world order, do you think I am going to sit down here, and run this revolution in line with these agents of backwardness, Religious strongmen and strongwomen in power at Abuja?, or the traditional rulers who are agents of the primitive age and anchored the people under over 5000 years of traditions and customs that influence the politicians according to the rule of the queen of England.

This revolution shall break every spirit of Pharaoh that refused to let my people go, and the people shall be free, let the freedom rain, any traditional ruler that prevent the release of the people from bondage and oppression with this revolution will go into exile and its palace shall be converted into museum and public library by the local government. In shall Allah. Let my people go, and let the freedom rain, They told me that I should not mess up the oil, I mess-up the oil, They said to me, I shall not mess up the boundary, but I have mess-up the boundary, then for 40 years they punished me, the son of the soil, I ran away to America for 12 years today, still they would not left me alone, but they still purse me here. But with all they did to me, I am still here to complete my purpose on earth.

They said noise should not be made about me, but because of me there are now noises in town, they said nobody should fight because of me, but see now the world are now fighting because of me, They said to me, I am but nothing, a commoner, an orphan, Mr. nobody, He is poor, where would he see money to do this, if we tight him down financially, but here I am today fulfilling my purpose without your donation or grant, someone in my family told the people that they should have sold me before this time and use the money realized from trading with my life as a price to buy a lamp, but see God, I have become in their very eyes someone surrounded with flash lights, all of you should gather against me, but if your gathering is not according to will of God for Nigeria. your efforts shall be in vain and you will end your life in disgrace, but if I have done this because of my ambition. you shall stop this, but if this is set up by the Almighty God using me as protagonist of this revolution to free the people of Nigeria. you shall see the beginning. but shall not partake of its harvest, because this vehicle is carrying me forward to victory over any deceptive family manipulation and traditional spiritual control mechanism. Every spiritual arrows shot against me is going back to their senders, Let the freedom rain, and let it rain, from Sokoto to Calabar remembering King Jaja of Opobo, let it rain, let it rain from the tomb of Amino Kano, let the freedom rain. And let us meet where the Benue river welcome the river Niger to become one river to water the destiny of a people and make 3 nations into one country and they become one family, one people, one God, one nation, one modern Nigeria. Where the power of the people is the power of its political and economic leadership. Don't you heard how the Owo masquerades sang a song about me in Yoruba as a motherless boy? **(Eni ti a bata ki a fi owo re ra atupa, to deni a Jin tan ina WO, Ayaya lode, ajin gbomo lose, Awawa o, Oma logho made.)**

There is no town like Owo, and there is no village like Isijogun, My mother was born in Owo and My father was born in Isijogun, blow the trumpet in Owo, Blow it in all villages. blow it in all hamlets and in all farmlands behind the Ogbese river, and tell my people to let the freedom rain, Let it begin now! Let the freedom rain. Let it rain. And blessed is that man that does not stumble because of me. the fact that I am a prophet that eats Akuta and Agbogboluju does not mean I am just like another John the Baptist that can be harassed by the Chiefs of my people, let the freedom reign. Let it rain.

REASON THREE FOR THIS REvolUTION

Nigeria size with approximately 140 million people with over 300 indigenous ethnic groups, 3 major languages of Yoruba, Hausa and Ibo speaking people, and large revenue petroleum exports make it significantly different from other developing nations in Africa. Nigeria as an oil producing nations with its vast human resources and the high level of education attainment by the Yoruba's, and the industrialist genius of the Ibo boys and peace, harmony, humility and hospitality of Hausa and Fulani women does not deserved a ration of $1 to the poor and $50 dollar to the rich in the national distribution of wealth to the citizen. This revolution will reverse that, do you have an understanding about what I am trying to say here, that one Nigerian has $50, and the next man living next door is given only one dollar, is that a good distribution system of distributing national wealth, and what the Muslim nations is telling the man with one dollar is rap yourself with bomb and kill yourself as a terrorist, so that God will welcome you to heaven, and the Pope through his catholic bishop is telling Nigerians we bring nothing to this world and we shall take nothing out of it, so Zion come to church and get donations for used clothes, and expired medicine donated to use by the Americans.

People are with lack of healthcare services, poverty is more felt in the North west, and the three northern areas with 65 percent, is not exempt from poverty, the northern elite build high walls around their mansion, while the 65% of northerners lives inside hurts with palm tree branches as roof sheets over their houses with no heat, this Northern dwellers who believe in Islam account to 35 percent of Gross domestic products (GDP) and they believe sincerely according to Islamic doctrine that if you are poor, God destined you to be poor, those who are rich, it is their destiny, so the Imam and the Alhajis are comfortable being richer in the midst of poverty of their own people because they have bound them with chains of Islam faith, so they continue to brainwashed the women with Islamic teachings, and use the stolen oil money to marry many wives. put black clothes to cover the women head and face. so that nobody will see the bruises of how they beat the women in domestic violence committed by their husband when the woman go out of the house. these northern women are subject to sharia laws, rules and regulations of Islamic faith and because this oppression of man by woman has go on for long, the women themselves have come to believe it's the right thing to do, because God commanded it in the Koran.

Alhaji is enjoying himself with abusive lifestyle against 4 women he cover-up their faces with head gear, and is now successful in using religious and family control mechanism to exclude the northern women from public participation of social, economic and political participation which is the right of every Nigeria women as it's also the right of all Alhajis and all Emirs and Imams.

This revolution will be build on the wake up of the northern women from the villages to the familiar urban centers, that day is coming says Allah, when Elehas no go gree, pulling off the cover, and match for their destiny, putting their children on the back of Donkey matching down to meet the do nothing half body naked Yoruba women at the market center, that day fertilizer will be sold for one Niara in the market, that day agricultural deforestation will stop, soil erosion, and desertion, and land will be protected as national park, and there will arise farmers in northern part of Nigeria that will grow enough rice not only to feed the nation, but have enough sufficient for export

Oil money contributes only 13 percent of GDP, and only one percent to agriculture, and oil trade only gives life survival to about one percent, and the entire 95% of women in the northern part of Nigeria lives in hunger with no nutritional food and clean drinkable water for themselves and their children, and upon this malady, Alhaji is still committing domestic abuse on these women in the name of Sharia and Islam teaching, do you think this will continue forever Emirs?.

This revolution shall create a national park in every state of the federation that shall not be control by the state governor or local government chairman, such national park shall be designated by this revolution as farmland for agricultural mechanized farming to feed the nation, and Nigeria from any part of the country shall be free to lives and work permanently in that national park, and the park shall be exempted from the influence of religion, and ethnicity, but a free land under the control of the federal government for people to grow food crops. livestock, and maintain a huge domestic and international market for their agricultural products, this national park shall be connected with adequate supply of transportation system to other part of the country with rail line. the rail line shall be build with fastest train to reach Abuja from any of the national park locations in one hour, there shall be modern drainage system. where shall we get the money to do this?. That is your problem, because what you don't know will kill you.

The reason why Nigeria is having problem is because of religion and ethnicity, separate that from Nigeria leadership, the people are blessed by God to do anything which they purpose in their mind to do if they unite as one in the spirit of nationalism, if they can have the confidence that if they invested in this place, and nobody is going to come and tell them to go, get away from my town, or get away from my village because you are Muslim and I am a Christian, or get out of my village because you are an Ibo and I am a Fulani woman, or you cannot sell or buy in Ibadan because you are an Ijebu woman, this revolution will build the spirit of nationalism in agricultural development by carving out designated land as National Parks in some state of the federation and the Mayor of such national PARK shall be elected with no regard to his/her ethnicity or religion affiliation, these cities shall be free from religious and ethnicity influence. a national city for the development of mechanized agricultural farms, iron and steel industries, and military equipments manufacturing plants, international schools and secularly sponsored international health care centers. A National Guard barrack and defense centers, and a local police that reports only to office of the President. A city free from the political control of the state governor in the state where it is situated. A home away from home for those who are in Diaspora who no longer fit into the tradition and customs and religious ignorant of the Nigerian people, a new city for new people who want to be free from the religion of our forefathers and their primitive customary and traditional ways of life that has crippled Nigeria development to a point where we may end up in a total democratic collapse scenario and a total breakdown of law and order that will lead to ouster of the present democratically elected government.

The religion and tradition institution leadership has now developed a crisis potential to occur in Nigeria, this problem was caused by last administrations, not by me, I never hold a political office in Nigeria, and there are no records that I got any contract from any state of the federal government, I was the Chairman / Managing Director of Tulalum Nigeria Limited for over 10 years but seek got no Aluminum contract from any state or federal governments during their housing boom era, so I am not part of this problem, that is why I am qualified to be part of its solution, this potential indicators in 2010 singly or in combination could peculate such a collapse of Nigeria, the collapse would dramatically scale back its engagement with present government and revert to a civil society takeover of government at both national and state levels, and the suspension of the current constitution will give way to a new revolutionary drafted constitution by the younger generations between the age of 18-62 years old, because Nigeria's political history since independence has demonstrated that the religious leaders and the traditional rulers contributed a lot to the collapse scenario which has brought us to where we are now, therefore instead for us to continue to run away from Nigeria to other countries of the world and become a second class citizen, or black monkey with green card and suffering for carrying the nationality name of Nigeria in our international passport, we have decided through this revolution to build a new cities. a national park carved out of some state to call our home, a city where there is no Oba, no Obi no Emir. No chief, no church, no Mosque, a new city operating in the realms of a new world order with liberty, freedom and justice.

A place to work, play and defend our liberty with justice among the committee of nations, and because nobody is bold enough to stand against these religious folks and traditional rulers who remains the custodian of poverty mentality in the midst of plenty, enough is enough, So help us God.

This is a revolution, it may looks to you that I am on crack cocaine, or mad, anyway it takes a crazy man to manage an Asylum like Nigeria, which means we shall have no regards to who own the land before its takeover, but its focus is unity for one destiny and it will best be done by the takeover of lands to be designated as national park for people anywhere to come, live and work, and builders from other parts of the world would be allowed to build houses for sale in these National Cities for the people who want to be free from religious and traditional control mechanism, people who have suffered abused because of religion. or by the tradition and culture of the elders shall move away from their places of birth and take permanent residency in the new world town, City of refuge with no traditional ruler or no approval permit for mosque or church buildings, people will travel out of the city in their own cars, buses or in train that are faster than their cars out of the cities to go and worship in their churches and mosques outside these cities, secular cities of freedom where religion is dead. But your faith shall remain a personal liberty, a personal relationship and your faith between you and your God. A city for those who want to work and play. But when you are ready to evangelize, take the next train to the other cities nearby, this is a National park for those of us who are ready to work and play in liberty and freedom. Let my people go, and let the freedom reign.

REASON FOUR FOR THIS REvOlUTION

The economy is stagnant because those in power in the last 40 years are the same people who always received the support of the traditional rulers, the Emirs, The Obis and the Obas political endorsements, and because this same people received the supports of the religious leaders like the Imams, and the Pastors and the Catholic Church land owners, they continue to be re-elected and rule the people in a way that at best was indifferent to the needs of the people and at worst flagrantly violated their human rights.

The Nigerian Electric power Authority (NEPA) is one of the highest cost producers of electricity in the world, 80 percent of firms have their own generators still in 2010, Nigeria has no plan in developing a nuclear energy to provide electricity to its 140 million population which will double to 270 million in another 10 years because if you ever sleep with a Nigeria woman, they give it to you all, you are working the sexual enjoyment alone and they are enjoying the act while fast asleep and coupled with the fertility of Nigerian women, this 140 million is going to double to 270 million in another decade, but United States concern is Nuclear power to fight terrorists who are in transit route though Nigeria, Air-ports, I have spent 12 full years in America, January 1, 1999-January 1, 2010 today that I am writing this book in my vacation resort, there has never been one full day for 24 hours that my light is off anywhere in US, this Nigeria revolution will order Nepa to remove their dams from river Niger and let the River Niger flow for irrigation to water the desert for mechanized farming to feed my people with no more importation of food from Ralph's stores to Nigeria.

I have about 135 million people living in darkness, they lack electricity to develop small business, you are talking to me about terrorism, the difference between me and you is this, you are building a nuclear power station in Nigeria to prevent the Terrorist to use Nigeria as a transit route to us here in America, fine, good idea, but this revolution has decided to take over your Nuclear power station and convert it to provide electricity to my people, can we have an understanding here?. And I know what you will do when it happened, you will call all your brothers together since all of you are the great grand children of the slave masters who build your nation with black slaves from Africa, sit down in emergency meeting in your security council created for the Security of you, by you and for you, Now let us placed sanctions on Nigeria, but my people will have electricity 24 x7, and use River Niger to irrigate our farms, food on our table, and lights in our homes. And all these young boys terrorist who are victims of your missionaries fake interpretation of the bible or the Koran will be converted to steel workers at Ajaokuta to use their knowledge to produce steel, without the supervision of the steel cartel from Russia, by then the Steel Cartel who has paralyzed Nigeria steel industry might have gone out of the Country by then, so these terrorist will have a job to do in this new nation, instead of working for Osama Bin Laden, for they will use local black smith method used in Nigeria 5,000 years ago before you discovered Nigeria through mungo park and Mary slessor.

This Ajokuta mamomi who are self made industrialist among us, represent our indigenous method of doing things, despite your sanctions to build a local rail line that will connect all states by train faster to reach Abuja in one hour from the National Park, or what job do you want a university graduate at 23 to do if he is unemployed in an oil produce country where your own interest is only the oil, gas and its timber? You are not interest in Nigeria people, all what you want is go there and get their god given natural resources by trick of negotiation, if you love Nigerians 140 million people, how did you demonstrate that love to me in my last 12 years in your village? You don't even believe that Tula is a complete human begins because of his black color and Nigeria accents. now you want to come here and tell me, how I solve my own problem?.

REASON Five FOR THIS REvOlUTION

The economy is growing at about 4%, while the annual population growth is about 3%. Nigeria food problem is caused by rural to urban migration an aging farming population with no children to inherit the profession of farming from their parents, because the focus of every child is to go to college, graduate and migrate to another countries, Farming as a profession lack appropriate technologies, including food storage and preservation system, lack of good transportation, market linkages, and problem of access to information to how food processing and packaging works, and lack of financial resources and services to small scale farming.

Timbers has gone from the forest, the wood exporters, lumber exporters, has deforest the national forest and ship the timbers out of the country, with no tree re-planting program, they took 90 tree from the forest and plant no tree for the coming generations, the money realized by these illiterate timber merchants and greedy timber exporters goes only to marrying of more wives, party, expensive imported clothes and cars, with no amount set aside to replace the timbers they removed from the forest, now this timber merchant has now put Nigeria to a deforestation to the point that 100% of the forest that existed in 1960 has now been reduced to 10%, what I mean is in my father's farm where there was 100 trees in 1960 by now in 2010 only 10 trees are left that has not been cut down. all the 90 trees were sold by my junior brother to timber exporter, below one dollar per tree, which means my brother was paid $90 for all the timber in the farm, and what did my brother did with the money? He used the $90 to buy a used motorcycle imported by the timber exporter from America, so at the end of the day the timber merchant got all the money, and he used all the money he made from exportation of the timber for housing project in America to import to Nigeria cars, clothes, and why doing a comeback from America party, he got another new wife at the party, and now he is fat with pot belly because of fufu, with few teeth left in his mouth because of bush meat, since he felt down 90% of the timber in the forest for exportation to make money, kill the animal in same forest for meat because he hate livestock like chicken and cow meat because it's from Fulani land, this typical Nigerian man has 14 children by 6 women and planted no single tree in the village to replace the 90 he cut to make money, despite the fact he is going to die very soon and left 14 children behind with deforestation problem in Nigeria, that is a typical Nigeria, how do you deal with this kind of elders in our society who has no future plan for the coming generations?. And this kind of people thought they are right and see you disrespecting the elders when you show them the truth, that is this revolution is inevitable, if the coming generation will want to have something left for them in Nigeria by the current leadership, so the time has come for a revolution, Let the surviving children of animals in the forest make a loud noise in the bush, the remaining children of leopard, the grass cutter, and the scoundrels and the Oketes who escaped the wicked bullets of hunter for bush meat shout in the forest and join the children of men for this revolution and let the freedom reign.

REASONSIXFORTHIS REvOlUTION

15 PERCENT OF Nigerian children die before reaching their fifth birthday these children are just victims of largely preventive illness such as malaria or diarrhea. Per capital income is $400 per year for about 10% of the population, while the rest 70% live under $1 a day, while 10% share the money generated from petroleum resources, and the rest 10% like me ran to other countries like America and begin to enjoy myself as a second class Citizen because of my black skin and Nigerian accent. And in Nigeria, the people there trusted indigenous institution such as age based community-based associations, the traditional rulers like the Emirs, the Obas, and the Obis, the religious leaders like their Bishops, the Pastors, the Prophets, these trusted leaders holds the power that determine whose candidates should be elected to political leadership position at both, state and federal levels, over and over again candidates connection or endorsement by religious leaders and traditional rulers determine the winner in all election, this system continue to perpetuate their personal interest rather than ideological platforms, thereby eroding opportunities for participation in political process and public leadership. because leadership are elected or appointed not on personal character and qualification for the job, but the and factors such as ethnicity, sex and age, how much money the candidates or applicant have can play with, the political process is crowded with control. intimidation of opponents, assassination, thug, poorly managed and rigging of election and patronage to religious and traditional rulers which has translated the legacy of the military past rules of poor maintenance of law and order. with corruption and lack of access to justice as a way of life of Nigerians.

80 percent of the women in northern Nigeria are illiterates, Nigeria massive unemployment problem and large numbers of tertiary graduates from the university remain jobless or end-up in the informal sector because the kind of education received in college does not equip young Nigerians for productive livelihoods, in the 1960`s and 1970s education is a way for the children of the poor parents could use to become upwardly mobile and move out of poverty, but in 2010, what education did to change the lives of the children of the poor parents no longer exist, thereby rendering Nigeria system a poverty dynastic, and the rich become richer while the poor become poorer or wealth dynastic, that means if your parents is rich, you will be rich, and if your parents is poor. you sure bet to be poor despite going to college, because the job is not there, or else get your visa and run out of the country to another countries.

REASONSeven FORTHIS REvOlUTION

Only slightly are half of school-age children attended school regularly and many drop out before completing primary school contributing to low adult literacy rates at 60% for men and 42% for women. Donors hate Nigeria because of Nigeria's oil wealth, Uganda for instance receive 50 percent of their recurrent expenditure from donor funds as compare with Nigeria who is just six percent donor funds, from donor standpoint, Nigeria is too important to ignore that is why we give them only this 6 percent to clean up their corruption, donors would not have made any donations to Nigeria at if not because it is too big to be ignore, and the programs and projects that attract donors to Nigeria are in the area of working with civil society group, rule of law, legislative assistance and elections. in all other area the attitude of donors is you have enough money to take care of your expenditure if you learnt how to manage your resources, or if you remove corruption from governance of your country.

Nigerian women many young and have an average of six children contributing to both a population growth rate that will double the population to 270 million in less than 15 years from now, how are Nigeria leader going to feed their children? With this high maternal morbidity that makes Nigeria women to 100 times more like to die of pregnancy-related causes than women in western countries. Law making bodies at both state and national levels are unclear on their mandates and do not function to effectively regulate or balance the powers of the executive. Characters of civilian politics in widespread use of patronage politics, corruption from top to bottom, and factional disputes among key personalities and their allies, and the frustration of Nigerians in Diaspora who are well educated, with good access to information does no longer fit in the local corrupt system of politics in Nigeria having live and work in developed nations of the world, and where they choose to stay abroad, the nationals of such nations lives with them with distrust because no other nations trust Nigeria again because of the bad records of get rich quick scam of some Nigerians who continue to go about from country to country duping everybody in order to make money and go back to Nigeria to assumed leadership position by bribing the Church Islamic and traditional rulers leadership for patronage to a political office.

The adoption of Sharia law into Nigeria constitution, which is among the greatest challenges for the legal development and reform of the justice system in the light of Moslem who now have access to western civilization ways of life.

The national assembly remain weak and uncertain of their roles in a presidential system they borrowed from America, because they continue to operates the legacy of the military, the legacy of the British system of government hand over to them by the Queen now interwoven with American presidential system of government they stole from United States, elections to the assembly and the executive branch of government were consistently flawed by poor administration and questionable practices every 4 years to return same people to office.

REASON Eight FOR THIS REvOlUTION

Patronage remains the customary way of conducting political business and civil society remains largely excluded from broad participation in policy, dialogue and setting the national agenda.

Low productivity, lack of competitiveness, an inconsistent policy framework and an unfavorable environment for investment and enterprise development that are stiffing the Nigeria economy which continue to make Nigeria bureaucracy to runs only on oil whereby petroleum exports account for about 90 percent of foreign exchange earnings, and over 70 percent of the federal budget, the bulk of which is expended on civil service and politicians salaries and allowances of appointed or elected officials, this petroleum is a capital intensive product now labor intensive at all, which created a scenario of mass unemployment because crude petroleum business can only create or give jobs to only one percent of Nigerians, this is how this thing work, petroleum gives 90 percent of income but it can only provide job for only 1 percent, which means 89 percent have no job. but to wait in line to get their portion from the 90 percent income, if you don't get it now, you get it later when this revolution begins in shall Allah, Nigerian youths are jobless and the adults have no work to do, no job but all play make Nigerians a poor rural country of jobless people, that is why they are religious fanatics. from mosques to churches, herbalist. prophets and witch doctors, to get money. despite the fact they do not work for money, and when they are demanding money from their brothers or sisters or parents in Diaspora phone can ring 100 times in a day, because the society has been program to believe that there is no other thing Nigeria can do to be rich without the petroleum resources, everybody abandon agriculture and stay put in urban centers doing nothing but want to eat, drink, party and go to church or mosque, and when the night comes. sleep and have sex. the end result more babies to double the population of do nothing people in another decade for 270 million people with dependence of oil only as a source to maintain the nation expenditure.

The dependence of oil business or dependency on crude oil as income for the past 4 decades has now put 70 percent of Nigerians in position of illegal aliens in Nigeria where they were born, because they have no access to quality of life like other Nigerians who manage the oil business

Women and minorities are particularly vulnerable to exclusion from political participation and in Nigeria 2010 women constitute only six percent of elected representatives at the national level. The gap between the rich and the poor is manifesting every day in large proportion with the wealthiest controlling 25 times more in comparable to the poor particularly with the women in the northern part of Nigeria, this disproportionately impoverished under the pretense of Islam has put women under a domestic abuse with their husband using the faith of Islam or sharia rules and law to perpetuate this domestic abuse and violence against northern Nigeria women who are largely low-input and low-output agricultural farmer to feed their family with no state welfare system from the state, a typical Nigeria woman in the northern part of the country is a Moslem, married to a shepherd or a low scale farmer in the rural areas. who is illiterate. lives less than a dollar a day, farm less than two hectares of land, employ only hand tools, and produces a very narrow range of crops. does deceive reliable extension of his farming advice, lacks information and linkages to financial services to expand his farm, produce jus less three quarters or less of household food requirement, next time the election comes, he vote he and his wife on religious consideration biased on what his emir want him to do, or his Imam directed him to vote, he has many wives and many children more than the crops of his farm, the only money he ever saved in his life is towards going to Mecca, and if the state could subsidized that, he will forever grateful for completing two pillars of Islam, married 4 wives and go to Mecca, but no plan for the 16 children born to him by these 4 women, all he is satisfied with is the title of Alhaji.

There continues social conflict despite 50 years after independence, conflicts triggered by resources competition, religious and ethnic differences, and the economic situation, these social conflicts unresolved has claimed thousands of lives over the past years, which now poses a major threat to stability in Nigeria.

There remain many roadblocks to strengthened Nigeria democracy because the political elites are enthroned, excluding most citizens, particularly women and the poor from manful political participation. God did not instruct Abraham on women genital cutting, but only for men pennies, but Nigerian continual cutting of women genital cutting has continues to increase the risk of death among many female. Nigeria is one of just five remaining nations on the surface of this planet earth who are polio reservoirs; all polio left other parts of the world and come to stay in Nigeria because Nigeria lacks a primary health care system to eradicate polio as it has be done in all parts of the world.

There exist a massive threat of HIV/AIDS in Nigeria and despite this USA and Nigeria relations is only strong only on oil and counter terrorism. HIV/AIDS is a growing menace in Nigeria, the country now accounts for nearly 10 percent of the HIV/AIDS burden in the world, which may double in 2012, and this disease is creating many orphans in Nigeria which is now about 2 million orphans in Nigeria in 2011 with no enough orphanages to cater for the needs of these children. Nigeria is a major malaria endemic country, out of the population of about 140 million, 50 million experiences episodes of malaria every year, despite the fact that malaria is preventive and mosquito has been wipe out in other countries, Nigeria still abhors mosquito as if all mosquito that was sent away from all part of the develop worlds flew to Nigeria to make the country as their new abode, because Nigeria seem to be a country that has no plan to eradicate mosquitoes that is the major cause of malaria that affect about 50 million of its citizen every year, despite the fact that malaria is treatable and curable. Malaria accounts for about 30 percent of all childhood deaths in Nigeria, and about 50 percents of inpatient admissions in heath facilities, if Nigeria focus on prevention of malaria and HIV/AIDS in its health care services, the people will maintain an 80 percent population of healthy people.

REASON NINE FOR THIS REvOlUTION

Nigeria has the fourth largest tuberculosis burden in the world, and the country has the highest number of HIV/AIDS orphan in west Africa, along with Ethiopia, china, India, and Russia, Nigeria is projected to be one of the five "next wave" countries that will double or triple the number of global HIV cases by 2011, HIV is transmitted by long-distance truck drivers who pick up ladies who are poor to afford transportation fares at toll gate expressway, or prostitutes who exchange their transport fare from one city to another for free sex with private car owners, also HIV's transmitted by uniform men like police officers who accept not only money as bribe. but also can accept sex with accused women as bribe, up to 70 percent of Nigeria prostates and single ladies today tested positive to HIV got it from policemen. because that is best way to eradicate corrupts police officer from Nigeria. give them HIV through sex with you as bribe.

Despite the civil society from military rule, Nigeria current leadership lacks capacity and financial resources it needs to truly engage with advocate for change, because the government has failed by and large to established partnership with citizens and the private sector actors, and therefore government institutions are confused by external forces beyond their control to carry out their own mandates to the people, hence there is no alternative to move forward than this revolution.

Over 50% of Nigerians still live rural areas and farm for a living with their hands and legs with no modern family tools, machinery and equipments, agriculture which provides a precarious livelihood, marked by decline productivity environment degradation and poor market linkages.

Financial institutions do not save farmers and rural entrepreneurs. Nigeria agricultural commodities such as cocoa and rubber are no longer competitive in regional or international market, farmers have moved from their local farming villages to urban towns seeking their cut in the distribution of petroleum dollars, agricultural products processing and technologies are readily available, the natural resource of Nigeria is agriculture, but this culture of the people lack market information and commercial orientation to farmers putting the remnants of Nigeria natural resource base at risk of extension, making Nigerians to depend on imported foods which now is eroding Nigerian farmers competitiveness in the world market, poverty and marginal growth of former farmers but now jobless with no modern skill as new urban dwellers is a great question that can only be answer by a green revolution agenda.

Nigeria is effective in providing quality social sector services to the people. In America there exist welfare social programs for the poor to provide food stamps, nutrition, health care services, and social support services to all who lack employment, but have children, but lack of this social services in Nigeria now results to high child maternal morbidity and mortality rate, no child supports to single women and divorced women, low level of adult literacy and poor academic performance and high fertility rate of Nigerian woman that continue to translate into rapid and unsustainable population growth.

A Nigerian woman dies every three minutes from causes related to poverty, lack of healthcare coverage related to pregnancy and childbirth. A significant national response to disease is very difficult to develop in Nigeria because of mass illiteracy, fear of rejection, discrimination and stigma associated with anyone with certain diseases and poverty, and being a large country with a serious HIV/AIDS problem there exist no sufficient programs by the federal government to support the treatment and eradication of HIV/AIDS, malaria and common fever in the country.

The poor quality of education coupled with lack of access to information is encapsulating successive generations of the poor deeper and deeper into poverty, if your parents were poor, you will definitely remain poor, because of the constraints to quality of education and access to information on how the system works.

The federal budget allocated low resources levels to health care, the most at risk population like uninformed personnel, the police, soldiers, prostitutes, truck drivers and orphans and vulnerable children that needed to be targeted for treatment, care and support interventions.

Nigeria food security operates in poor policy environment and low productivity, its conflict on religion between the Christianity and Islam and a host of other factors has transform the country into a low-income, food deficit country because the citizens cannot move from their native village to other part of the country without being treated like a foreigner in their own country, that is an Ibo man cannot travel to Kano to farm, and to address food insecurity in a nation, there must first exist the spirit of nationalism, the conflict in Nigeria at the moment in 2010 is localized. its disruptive effects threaten food security and income generation for the local farmers from other part of the country, even among Yoruba, the ibadans will still refer to the ijebu with 20 milies difference as a foreigner because they belongs to different ethnic groups, because there are about 300 ethnic groups with over 300 languages, if you do not remain to farm where you are born, but moved to other part of the country, you cannot get a land to develop any agricultural production, the local people outside your own ethnicity group will always see you as illegal alien in your own country, this primitive idea against nationalism is rooted in the blood of Nigerians, that is why Nigerians in dispora still carry that foundation believes to where they live in many parts of the country, organizing their own association and fellowship along ethnic groups.

Nigeria still operates under unsustainable system of natural resources, unplanned urban development, and obsolete petroleum industry operations which threaten availability of portable water and wood fuel, there continue to exist in Nigeria in 2010 unregulated urbanization that now poses enormous problem of sanitation and waste disposal, with flooding of the cities in every raining season.

Nigeria is pregnant with unemployed, ripe for conflict because the oil companies have damaged the environment and individual livelihoods, these oil companies has specifically contributed to the conflict environment if something is not done quickly to address these pregnancy for conflict, for this conflict that will soon develop to a national scale not to break Nigeria into pieces that will bring us back to the primitive age in the 21st century, there is no alternative to a revolution that will give birth to nationalism under one people with one aspiration for the benefit and the freedom of all.

Nigeria is pregnant with unemployed, ripe for conflict because the oil companies have damaged the environment and individual livelihoods, these oil companies has specifically contributed to the conflict environment if something is not done quickly to address these pregnancy for conflicts.

This revolution will address this pregnancy to give birth to a baby that will benefits and address the problems we face as a people. There is no political solution at hand by the present administration to address this conflict than a Nigerian revolution, the time for it is now.

Nigerian does have a resource of its own, of which he can seek justice and rights of its own people in this revolution, and no longer would this county operates under the harassment and bully of other nations, Nigeria human resources if rightfully use is competent as experts in a working partnership with other nations or go it alone in this revolution, for the manipulation of Nigeria by the world powers into submission is soon to be over, the human and natural resources of Nigeria will be use by this revolution to benefits and protect Nigerian people, faith based organization, the church leaders, Islamic leaders, the guru marajis. the traditional rulers that has help very powerful influence in deciding the political wave and direction of Nigeria elections and sit in position to endorsed the winner of their chise will take a back sit as custodian of the people culture and tradition and custom with the local government museum officials, the modern nation that will arise out of this revolution will not toe the line of a modern nation in the new world social order, that is above the regions mentality of Islamic leaders and the sharia laws, the revolution shall be a separation of state from religion. a secular state that has no base for the obis, the obas and the emirs in the directing the pace of elected officials, this revolution will only reports to one supervisor, the will of the people, a government that is accountable only to the electorates, because the political system as it now operates is manipulated by the traditional rulers with their native thugs, and the religious leaders who continue to make victims of Nigerians with their faith and religion, every Nigerian will be allow to serve God in their own way based on the kind of religion they choose, but we shall remain a secular system of government, in order to allow the 70% of Nigerians who currently remain in poverty to survive the new world order. riding very fast to new one world government, this revolution cannot afford any further the delay of Nigeria to join the train of the forces of the new world order, it's here, this is the time, the people must be free from this religious mentality and ethnic conflict, and ignorant of how the world operates, we cannot sacrifice the destiny of this nation on the altar of life after death, this is our planet, we shall live here in freedom and liberty for the few years that God has given us to inhabit this place, and we will leave it better for our children, a situation where 70% now lives in poverty is not acceptable to this revolution, Let the freedom reign, and let the ones in Diaspora come back home, let the Andrews that check out be back, and let us build this fallen wall together for the coming generation, some will give some, and some will give all, but at the end of the day, next generations shall remember us as the greatest of Nigerians ever live on this planet. Come back with your skill guys, and let the freedom reign.

THE Spiritual Allegory OF THIS Revolution

God stand in the congregation of the mighty; and judge among the gods, I have said, Ye are gods; and all of you are children of the most high, but ye shall die like men, and fall like one of the princes. PS: 82: 6-7.

For God sit in THE CONGRAGATION OF THE MIGHTY; AND HE JUDGE AMOUNG THE GODS, God rules and make judgment among the gods, and any god in the heavenly places that disobey the almighty God by seeking to be worship by men whom God has created, he demoted such god to the position of an angel to be servants to the children of men who are heir of salvation, and if they made such a mistake the second time, his judgment is to send them to the earth planet so that they can die as men. Because the gods and the angels are spirits, in other for them to die, they have to be demoted to become men. Because only the children of men can die and then be judged and go to hell.

When some of these former gods or angels took the body of men and come down in human flesh to our planet earth, they quickly forgot whom they were, and failed the temptation and tests presented to them from Satan who is the god of this world, this gods in human flesh will then got carried away and enticed by the love of vain glory and materialism, these gods among us becomes afraid of men, forgetting that they are gods sent down by God for a specific purpose here on earth, and because they fear man, and seek the approval of man, and want to be political correct with the children of men, want to have good reputation, and retire with millions of dollars in their private bank accounts, they end up in failing to fulfill their purpose and assignment here on earth, and then die like men and end up in hell just like Satan that deceived them.

These dwell among us gods in human flesh end up using their gifts, talents, power and anointing and calling upon their life to acquired wealth, that is, if one thousand are sent to your country, only one will pass the test of the flesh to do what he came here to do, the rest 999 will end up with a lot of stolen money and women to enjoy their short life span and then they will die like men. (That suggests to you that there are not less than one thousand Nigerians qualified like me to lead this revolution, but where are they since 1960 Nigeria independent? Or do you want to tell me that God never sent a leader that will solve Nigeria to us in the last 50 years? and those who has been prepared by God right now, are afraid to rise up, because they do not want die, or their wife is telling them, you can't do this, or they already ran away to become a citizen of another country, or they right now at Abuja or in some remote Nigeria state legislature or in the executive arms of government acquiring wealth to themselves. taking their own cut from the national cake. Forgetting who they are, and that rise it is appointed unto a man to die once, after this come judgment.

The gods and the angels cannot die, the only way they can die is for God to send them on assignment to this our planet, be deceived by Satan the god of this world, die and then end up with Satan in hell, but the few wise among the gods who are here on assignment, and know whom he or she is before this earth planet is laid on the surface of ocean care less about what you say or think or write about them, your criticism and opposition of their assignment, men opinion cannot stop them, oppression, sanctions. sufferings, hunger, loneliness. sickness, or whatever you do to them will only result at the end of the day to build them into a character that will strengthen them and give them the kind of life experiences they need to accomplish their purpose on earth, because they know whom they are before the foundation of the world, these few men knows that after their short life span. there is more to this life, which is life eternal, those ones, is the type of gods that will not die as men, but will return back to their original place in Heaven after completing their assignment here on earth, because they seek no man approval or honor or bi-partisanship, in achieving their purpose to benefit mankind.

The ones that rejected Satan temptation to lure them away from their destiny by beautiful women, love of their own children, acquisition of mansions, cars, boats and private jets, these sons of God among us through suffering, persecution and opposition will remained focus to accomplish their purpose on earth.

A nation that kill or prevent such a god in human flesh sent to them will have to wait for another 40 years, for another one to emerge in such a country for their deliverance, Because it takes God about 20 years to make a man in conformity to his purpose on earth, learning about his environment, his people, acquire enough knowledge and life experiences before he surely understand his or her purpose in this planet, so if you kill the one sent to your village, your state, your family or your nation, it does not bother God, because it is you that will lose and would have to wait for another one to emerge, and if the another one is born in your country today as a baby girl or boy, the process of manhood making begins at the age of 12, add 20 years making of satanic temptation. errors and omissions for character formation process, which means you may have to wait till 2042 to get another opportunity like this, and by then most of Nigeria pressmen and women or the elected officials in both the executive. legislature and the judiciary now in 2010 might have die and be in heaven or in hell in 2042.

The above spiritual allegory is why I am calling on all Nigerians born between 1950 to 1990 to purchase this book and read it, if you are a publisher or an editor or author, translate it in major Nigerian languages of Yoruba, Hausa and Ibo and distribute it to Nigerian people, to take the message of this book very serious, wherever they are in any part of the world, at home and abroad, you know whom you are, for this purpose some of you are born. Fire-up wherever you are hiding now, Get-up and get ready to go, the time for the freedom of Nigeria people has come, let the freedom reign and let my people go.

For me, by the power of God anointing and calling that is upon my life to lay the foundation for this revolution, let it be known to all men and women, to all races and all residents of this planet that the words that flows here from the barrel of my pen shall accomplished all what I sent it to accomplish for the people of Nigeria, and no single drop of the words of this book shall pass away without accomplishing what I purposed it to accomplished, the past years of civilian electioneering campaign slogan from the day of Olu Falae presidential election during the time of acting head of state General Adulsamai Abubakar and Obasanjo who was released from house arrest after the death of Abacha. in June 1998, the political slogan of Nigerian political aspirants has always been change!, change!!, change!!!, but my campaign for this revolution in Nigeria is not Change. keep the change that is my tip for you for serving me a bad meal, I do not need change, because no man or woman can change his or her attitude, character or disposition after the age of 40, Any elected officials in Nigeria government today in the Executive or legislative assembly who are over the age of 60 will not change the status quo, that is why when the law enforcement arrested someone, they look at your age, and your past records, if you have committed certain crime after the age of 40, got bail out, and you go ahead and commit similar crime second time after the first one. and now you are caught again for same crime the third time, and you were over the age of fifty. three strikes occurred on same type of crime?. You need to go to jail, you elected someone in power at the age of fifty, he did bad, you re-elected him again at 54, he did bad, and at 58, you put him back there?. And now he is in your house crying I will change, change, change, no, you cannot change because you are already 62 years old, so these people are not going to change, they have become dried fish, what you do this time is to vote them out of office, all of them, both at the states and federal level, I do not want your change, it is the politicians that trade with the lives of 140 million Nigerians in their buy and sell in the political market place that talk about change, Nigerians are not for sale, so we don't need your change, all what we need now is a revolution, because I want all what the devil has stolen from Nigerians back, not the change. Let my people go!. And let the freedom reign.

They sold Nigerians in the world market as commodities, so every election time they promise the electorate to give them change, How much did you give to us or pay us in the last 4 years that you are asking us for change, But for me, since I have no political experience in the trade of selling Nigerians to make money like this political aspirants, and since I know that Nigerians are not for sale to the highest bidder with more money than commonsense, all I am saying is Give me all, not the change, do not pay us with checks, because in the last election you gave us checks with a promising note, and when we took your check to the bank, your checks bounced. This time you need to come back home; we need another person to represent us there. Thank you for your service, keep the change as your tip, for being a bad waiter or waitress. Let the freedom reign.

This time we vote for no change but to the People Revolution of Nigeria Let my people go and let the freedom rain. Let it rain, let the Elehas removed the black covers garment from their face, and put their children on the back of Donkeys and match from every villages and hamlets of Sokoto, Kano, Kaduna and Maiduguri down to where river Niger met with river Benue, and let us use these days to give an answer to the national questions, Let the half naked women from Calabar and Enugu market, joins hand with the Edo women, and remember on their way to wake up from sleep and slumber the do nothing beautiful Yoruba women and let us all meet at that place where two rivers joins together in unity to become one river and flow together to the Atlantic Ocean watering the destiny of this nation on their way to the sea and let the freedom rain. Let it rain because of 15% of Northern Nigerian children that die before their fifth birthday, these children are just victims of largely preventive illness such as malaria or diarrhea which has been eradicated in countries with similar output of oil like Nigeria, Let the freedom rain. Let it rain. Some will give some, some will give all, but at the end of the day my people shall be free. And at the end of the day our children shall remembers us in history as the best generation that ever lives in Nigeria. Let it rain.

OlUSEgUN OBASANJO & USMAN YAR` ADUA

Nigeria is the most disappointing nation in adopting democracy in Africa; Olusegun Obasanjo was imprisoned because of his public condemnation of the regime of Sanni Abacha corruption and human rights abuses, but after the death of Abacha, in June 1998. Obasanjo was supported or influence by the west to seek the presidency. while at the same there are other faction from the west that supported Olu Falae, a graduate of Yale University and former finance minister to run for the presidency.

Nobody becomes Nigeria presidency under a ballot box without being supported by the west, I was at AME Church in Los Angeles on Sunday morning shortly after the release of Mandela of South Africa from prison and his visit to America, in my presence members contributed to his presidential campaign about one million in a day, that was how a man who spent 27 years in jail got money for his campaign to become the president of south Africa, and where did Obasanjo got money to contest election to the presidency after spending 2 years under house arrest by Dr. Abacha, where did MKO Abiola got money to get a mandate of the people he never claimed, so the provision in Nigeria current Constitution that candidates may not receive campaign donation from outside the country is just to perpetuate this secret agenda to leadership by the elite. that is why every politician wants to get as much millions they can get secured in their bank account now, so that next election they have money to pay their thugs, I will get money from anywhere the money is to· run you guys out of town. That is why I went and did a short evening course at University of Los Angeles—UCLA Extension on fundraising, I never stole Nigeria government money before like you guys, so I will raise money from private Nigeria individuals anywhere in the world to support this revolution in order to be empower to run you out of town, if you want to stop this movement of the people, you feel me now?, because I am not playing with you, now that we have an understanding, there is not going to be a fight between us, right?. Deal.

The reason for this revolution is that we the people did not go to Military college to major in the subject of Coup planning and election rigs with minor in farming and machine gun repair mechanic like you my Uncle. therefore I am calling on all Nigerians in Nigeria and all Nigeria in Diaspora irrespective of any provision of the electoral commissioner, all individuals Nigerians that support the idea of this revolution should contribute either 100 US Dollars, 100 British pound sterling, or 1000 Nigeria naira each person, in order to raise the needed money for the D day, hope my Uncle will help us with a bag of Launch when we match through pass his Ota farm on our way to freedom square at Aso Rock. but don't forget that Uncle was the Commander of 3rd marine commando, so be careful boys and girls.

There was a wide disparity between the number of votes observed at the polling station and the final results that have been reported from several states, because the state governors, many of them former army generals, had decided that their fellow Army officer Olusegun Obasanjo should be elected and therefore they took actions by manipulation of the elections to ensure victory for Obasanjo. and despite Olu Falae presentation of his proof of fraud to the electoral commission, and the federal courts, his claim was rejected.

In 2003 it becomes obvious that Obasanjo despite his criticism of Abacha regime was only able to achieve few reforms, despite the failure in his first term in office, he was re-elected again with 61.8 percent of the votes under a fraudulent election condemned by the European Union, the national democratic Institute and international election monitoring teams.

In 2007, President Obasanjo sought to have the constitution amended to permit him a third term in office, but surprisingly the independent national assembly refused to rectify the change for him, this Baba Ota, put Umaru Yar ` Adua, a relatively unknown Muslim governor of a remote northern stated in power, a very gentle, honest, sincere man, but ignorant about the game of the new world order, but was elected anyway, with the same way Obasanjo was elected, that is how Obasanjo laid a terrible example for other African countries on how to become a president of a nation through a fraudulent election, and all these three elections that put

Obasanjo in power for two terms and Yar ' Adua were all condemned by both local and international observers.

Mind you this Obasanjo joined the Army when he was 21 years old, and came back to Ota his town at the age of 42 years old as a former head of state of Nigeria, for your political understanding, Obasanjo at 42 has already attained a position of former Nigeria president, can you see how far a man with minor in machine gun repair mechanic can move in life achievements, so all his life, Obasanjo has been enjoying and get paid on government pay checks, having served before then as the Vice to Murtala Muhammad, which means this Baba Ota ruled Nigeria for not less than 40 years directly or indirectly, the only time he lost control of Nigeria was when Abacha was in power, again don't forget that through him as Commander of 3rd marine commando. the Biafra Army handed over the civil war.

Obasanjo was born to lead, he and Murtala Muhammad were gods sent to Nigeria by the Almighty God, but how does Obasanjo lead us in the plan of God for his life and this country?. He end up giving us checks, but when we took the check to the bank, the check bounced.

I have seen the affliction of my people, and I have come down to deliver them from their enemies, says the lord, all what the people need to do is to match around this wall for 100 days, and all the wall of Jericho will fall down, that day my people will be set free, let the freedom reign, let it rain, let it be said to our children that one day in Nigeria history, a generation stood up and fight not for themselves but their children children, that is how the people of river Niger area build a nation of freedom and liberty. let it rain people.

The truth of Nigeria leadership is simple, those who are criticizing the youth of today actually took over Nigeria leadership through the barrel of gun between the age of 21-30 years old, Gowon was about 30 years old when he became Nigerian Head of State as a bachelor who get hook with Victoria a nurse on hospital state visit as head state, now at my age, Who is that bastard or Agbaiya in Nigeria that will tell me that I have no right to write this book? Or seek the leadership of Nigeria at this juncture?, who? no Nigerian has more right to Nigerian leadership that I do, Nigeria leadership is not for sale. it is the right of every qualified Nigerian irrespective of his or her religion and state of origin, so I am accepting the leadership of this revolution with no pretence. and no apology to any Nigerian in Nigeria or in Diaspora, because this is what I am born to do.

Therefore I wrote this book with no apology to any Nigeria at home or abroad, I am a Citizen of Nigeria with no less a right to Nigerian leadership just like Obasanjo and Yar` Adua, Yar` Adua second time in office, will be a disaster to Nigeria progress in the 21st century, therefore I am calling on all Nigerian youth of today between the age of 18-30 years old, to come out from their closet and join me to re-build this nation for them, from these selfish elders, all what the youth of Nigeria want is to run away from Nigeria to overseas, you do not want to fight for your own rights as a citizen, but what you want is to line up in millions at British and United Sates embassy for visa applications, therefore you these young boys and girls in Nigeria is wasting your own generation, if you refused to rise up now. through this revolution from the grass root, to safe your future from these elders who care not about the future generations of their own children, but want to employ the tradition. custom and religion of respect your elders to discourage you through their own locally made propaganda to stop you from allowing them to destroy your future. therefore, Are you fire up? Are you ready to go?. then let the freedom rain, and let it rain, from college and university campuses across the land, from the labor unions, and from the market women supporting their children. from Churches and the Mosques, let us have the D. DAY OF FREEDOM. And let the freedom rain.

Begin this revolution in your family meeting get together, and make a suggestion on how your family can be better, there you will learn that all these elderly people will tell you stories about how they have been doing this thing like this way, with this system of traditions and customs and our religion before they brought your mother to this house.

I am your mother, I am your father. if you want to talk to me you have to kneel down, prostrate right now, you don't talk to elders like that, and who are the elders?. the elders are those who led a civil war when they are 21-24 years old, they are the elite elders now are telling a man at my age. that I have no say in the affairs of the state?. The devil is a lair, let the freedom rain.

You became the head of state of this country at the age of 30, by then you were a bachelor, now you are telling Tula who has children under $1 a day job with a university degree?. About experience in Nigeria leadership position?. what did you know at the age of 29 when you became our head state?, nothing than drinking beer at the officers mess, even at that age, you did not even know how to talk to women. that is why you did not even have a wife before you became an head of state, until you use your office fiat to get one at my home town hospital at Ibadan. anyway when I need a wife. I will contact you to know how to use your system to get one after this revolution, because me too is still single like you. Blessed are the elders and the elite of Nigeria that don't make these youth of Nigeria angry during the D-day of this revolution. In shall Allah.

All the problems of conflict we are having right now in Niger Delta area has answers in the proposal presented by the youth of Niger Delta Community, and the Ijaw youth militant group.

These intelligent young leaders proposed from time to time for solution but Obasanjo and Yar` Adua with their 40 years reign in Nigeria, has no solution yet, and I know now they already have plan for 2011, so that Obasanjo can continue his role as the leader behind the scene, Ijaw young people were accurate in their predictions of Nigeria oil business, and nobody listen to them, and how long will Nigeria youth play away their future?. let the freedom rain and let my people go.

Every Nigerian youth everywhere seek nothing today but an inner peace that comes from their right to voice their views, choose their leaders, feed themselves, get marry, take care of their families, and raise healthy and educated children, but the way Obasanjo/Yar` Adua establishment is messing up Nigeria now, if those of us born between 1950-1990 in Nigerian failed to act now, the coming Nigerian generations will curse us as a generation of coward, selfish and self centered individuals, who blow up all the resources on vanity lifestyle and vain glory. generations that cut down all the timbers in the forest. export them overseas. and plant no tree for the coming generations, generations that kill the animal in the bush for bush meant and developed not enough livestock farms for the coming generations, generations that ran away from home and left their own children to suffer. but get financially secured in Diaspora and forget to develop a nation for their own children children. that is why Obasanjo and Yar` Adua cannot stop this revolution, for it will not required army take over, so don't bother to service your old outdated military equipments. because this a revolution of national widespread that the people will know it's their own revolution, they will start it, and they will sustain it, then all Nigerian will own it, so that there will no more in the land be any conflict or violence on religion and ethnicity.

That day has come, it is now, let the freedom rain and let it rain. I have sound the trumpet, let the people that hear it launch the mass movement from this day from every corner in this country and let us give answers to the age long national questions that nobody is bold enough to answer, this is the day that the Lord has made, let us rise up and rejoice in nationalism, and come together as a people and get our freedom at last, let the freedom rain everywhere, from every mountain tops down to every valley, let the freedom rain, let it rain.

Nigerian CHRISTIANS

I am writing this last chapter of this book today January 1st, 2010 after doing my prayer alone in my bedroom for the new year, missing for the first time of my life in the last 40 years an annual rituals of spending the end of the year in a church.

Nigerians Christians spend their 31st December to 1st January of every year in Churches, that is why I drove yesterday afternoon around the nearby cities near this my vacation resort location to identified a church where I will celebrate my usual vigil which has been my ritual and traditions in the past 40 years, every new year 1st of January must see my presence in the church. A second after 12 midnight of every December 31st, I will be set for the pastor to lead the Happy new year shout.

But the year 2009 31st to 2010 1st, is different today because all the 10 churches and various denominations buildings that I identified in this white man city yesterday did not open for the usual night vigil ritual of 31st December 2009 to next day January 1st, 2010, a reason I prayed, and did my night vigil alone by myself in my bedroom.

The only Church that open was filled up with Christian youth party, and since these 2 cities around me here are white man land, no single black man or woman lives in these 2 cities except me who is here on vacation, despite the fact that 13% population of Americans are blacks, and despite the fact that these white Christian men do not pray and observe special days rituals of 31st December to January 1st every year, nobody lives in this city where I am now writing this book with no cars, nice house with less than 5 bedrooms, then I wonder, why are they blessed despite the fact that they are Christians that observed no special days or any rituals associated with special days of the month and year?. Why are they blessed for not dancing in churches?. Why are they bless despite the fact they do not pray? Why do these white guys have all they need and live a comfortable life and there is no poverty here in this city?. They go to church one day in a week, and in their church, they don't know how to dance or shout, just fellowship in scripture and that is it? Don't you have any enemy to pray against?. Then it occurs to me that most of my prayer is because of my foundational heritage as a black man and poverty dynastic. And the environment that I grew up, and the country I was born. And the type of leadership we have in Nigeria in the last 40 years.

The white men works 6 days a week, go to church one day a week, and go on vacation to play, but Nigerians don't work, they all left their farmland, abandon the villages and choke themselves in Ajegunle trading in tokunbo products in urban towns, because they have crude oil?. And their sons, daughters, brothers and sisters, fathers and mothers, uncle and nephews that ran abroad must send them money from overseas.

And we Nigerians in Diaspora pray a lot too, because being in America is like fighting a Biafra—war, you are constantly in arms way of losing an opportunities to a Mexican who is white and can speak English and Spanish, so every day you experience being deny an opportunities you are more than qualified for, because you are a Nigerian, you have a black skin, and your Nigerian accent, where are from?. you will answer them Nigeria, then his second question, Ibo?. Yoruba? Or Falaani,? or Abusa? Or Sekerri: you answer Ibo, now they will quickly take a step backward from you, and hold on tight to their purse or handbag, as if the judge has issued 10 yards restraining order between them and Nigerians. and this has led some Nigerian abroad to deny being a Nigerian nationals, then your family members you left at home, do not want you to come back to Nigeria again, because they want to be living in your house free without payment of rent, and it is you that will still send them money for Nepa bills?. But here you are as second class citizen, treated like a monkey with a green card, an object to fear, and distrust because some of the Biafra boys who ran overseas in the 70s have become internet crooked, and the beautiful Yoruba women hate to marry non Nigeria, but marry one anyway to get green card and has become a and terrorists to the man she was forced to marry for green card. now in 2010 the young Nigerian Moslems as become terrorist. and the rest of us good boys with Nigerian diploma. degrees and certificates we brought from Nigeria realized that all our certificates is but a piece of paper not recognized in the land, so until you work 18 hours a day, go to school 4 hours or go to school online while sleeping on your computer to have their own certificate in their own school, we cannot be employed. so the only thing you can do now is get your guard card, or nursing assistant certificate, be our security guard, take care of the sick. the mental patients and wash our toilets, because the blacks American here no longer want to do these kind of job again since we free them as slaves, so these jobs don't care about your color or accent or Nigerian nationality because you have no access to cash which they considered if they put Nigerian in position with collecting money he will run away with the money, so work and get your paycheck, and be sending money to your people back home in Nigeria.

Now come to we Nigerians in Nigeria that have someone living abroad, if we asked you for $1,000, and you don't send it to us right now, your phone will be ringing 1000 times today, in order for you to know that we are impatient with you. because all these phone calls. count it. we are deliberately doing it to let you know that every dollars we demanded from you represent each phone calls until you send your pay check, or get a loan from your credit card company. because we have a party coming up this weekend, a funeral of a rich man who has no life insurance to cover his or her burial expenses, left nothing for the children except a farmland he already made a bush meat of all the animals and sold all the timber to Balogun Sawmill, and if you don't send it on time. or you send us only

$250, you will be punished for it through our witchdoctors, because from the $250. we would spend $50 from Celestial and Cherubim and Seraphim prophets, and to Alfas and witchdoctors to punish you, so that when next you come back to this planet, you will learn how to go and work in that battle ground and remember your people back home, so you are struggling over there facing every opposition and human degradation as an immigrant, and instead for your family back home to be praying for you as Christians. here they are placing curses. jinx, spells on you in the battle ground, are these the Nigerians you call Christians with title in Nigerian churches?. Someone who is praying against his own family member in the battleground of survival?. When Americans sons and daughters are in war front, American Christians bring the picture of their soldiers to churches for prayer, to pray for their protection and to come back home, winning the war, but Nigerians at home take the pictures of their own family in Diaspora to satanic prophets for negative prayers, so that they don't come back home again, but should die overseas. Are these people you call Christians? Because they dance, sing, pray, and go to church in open stadium under rain and sunshine?.

The white guys always ask me, why are you paying too much like this?. What is the problem with you? And I usually give them one answer;

that All statistic about religion of Christianity and Islam in Nigeria are false, the truth of Nigerians religion are 30%Muslim, 15% Christians, and 55 % Satanism. The Ibo and Yoruba are nations with over 5000 years history in the mythology of Satanism, occultism and demonism, because every Yoruba or Ibo child is born into an ancestral burdens, foundational contamination with evil rituals, satanic family inheritance, ancestral yokes, and burdens, unprofitable spiritual family heritage control mechanism, this issues is in their blood wherever they go, and these also affects all the black slaves that was brought to America, who are now African American, therefore any black man anywhere in the world is affected negatively in the spiritual realm not by act of his character. which manifest physically in their slow economic advancement in the global market, so a black man problem is not about him? it is about his age long spiritual foundation, since Nigerian understand that fact, that is why they pray too much and not like the white guys.

The truth about Nigeria religion and faith is rooted in Satanism, great evangelist, bishops and pastors here in America always come back to us in America after they visited Nigeria for crusades with reports that Nigerians are the best Christians on earth, because the way they dance, pray, and stay in open sun and rain to attend their crusade, but what these missionaries don't understand is the fact that Nigerian Christianity and Islam is rooted in Satanism and wickedness, hatred of one another, even the church people that claim to be born again, You should go to any Nigerian church for our prayer meeting, you will witness the kind of anger we display in prayer, die, die, die, I say. die, die. die, right now fall down and die, die, die. die. be impotent, be paralyzed die.die, in the name of Jesus die, I say die. Who is she playing against?. May be her husband, or mother in law, or co-worker, or a business associate, and the problem that she is trying to spend 3 days fasting, sleeping in the church, going to mountain for prayers may just be something caused by the bad choice she made in life due lack of information about how the economic system operates, or as a result of being an illiterate, or lack of social skills, pride, un-forgiving spirit, now she want God to help her kill somebody?.

Moslems too use same method justifying themselves that this is the way of Allah, political opponent assassination is now the order of the day in Nigeria led by those who claim to be Muslim. those Alhajis who are ready to kill other family member because they disagree with his/her political manifesto or he want to win the election at all cost, now hired a hire-killer to kill his opponent, is this a man your statistics call a Moslem, A Moslem that will sit on prayer mat or leopard skin mat to issue jinx and spells on other member of his family?.

It is America who fear terrorist, we in Nigeria see our own family member as terrorists trying to kill us, that is why we go to church and pray hot prayer for God to rain fire from heaven and burn them beyond first degree burnt. I remember when I used to go to mountain top to pray, Fire, Fire, Fire, holy ghost fire consumed them, now, now, now, now, now, die, die, die in Jesus name, Amen. The kind of energy you should have use to be a great bricklayer, here you are using it at this mountain of fire, only to end up as poor man because you have no job.

For us to move forward in Nigeria, we would have to accept the truth through this revolution to adopt a secular state, and let religion be a private matter between man and his God, because as long as we give consideration to a religion affiliation to pick our leaders, or a geographical place of birth to be a relevant consideration to elect or appoint a leader, this united front to make Nigeria a great country may end up in error of history.

Any provision in the current constitution that recognized religion of Islam and Christianity as a state religion, or respect the traditional rulers Involvement in Nigeria politics should be removed and any nation in history that accomplish this task of separating religion from the state and its traditional rulers from the control of elected officials has always achieved such goal through a revolution of the people, because no elected Nigeria leader can promised to deliver that in the current national assembly, but a revolution that involved the people from the bottom up, is what we need now in Nigeria, therefore my people I have done my part, and hereby drop my pen, go ahead and let the freedom reign, and free yourself. When you need me, you know where to come and get me.

THE PRAYER OF CHAIRMAN Tula

Thank you Lord for giving me the privilege. grace, mercy, protection, opportunity. provision luck, the spirit of obedience, wisdom, knowledge, understanding, time, divine health and blessing to do my part in this revolution, I wrote 3 books before this one to complain the kind of hardship I went through in life but at the end of the day. you God put all the pieces together to make me and shape me into a character of a vessel unto honor fit for your use, and everything works for good at the end of the day, and I am so grateful for your sustenance and the spirit of endurance to go through suffering as a motherless baby from 1964 to this day, a life of lowliness that depend only on you in my day by day for survival, no mother no wife but I am still here in perfect union with your spirit, you saw me through all life difficulties and shameful experiences, bad choices that I have made in the past and bad mistakes that prepared me for this great task, Now I understand better that my character flaws was set by you to live among men in humility, and you opened my eyes to see what you want me to see, open my ear to hear what you want me to hear. From this day Lord give me understanding far above my teachers. the Elders, the Nigeria establishment, the elite the media, and west and east agenda, and let the mediation of my heart. and the words of my mouth and the words that flow out from the fountain of my pen come from your spirit for these great people. as I drop my pen this day having completed the last chapter of this book, let your name be glorified as you accomplished every word of this book to end the suffering of your people Nigerians and come down to deliver them from their oppressors and their evil task masters,.

I own no army, no gun. and have no tool or weapon of war beside my mouth and my pen and a wisdom that come from God to win this war for my people, therefore if it is possible that this thing can be done with no violence, because you God hate violence, let your name be glorified, but if we have to fight. gather your army from the remnant of your people this day and give us the victory over our enemies for it is you that rules in the kingdom of man, for thou is the kingdom, the power and thy glory, forever and ever Amen.

Chairman Tula

www.ingramcontent.com/pod-product-compliance
Lightning Source LLC
Chambersburg PA
CBHW072338290526
45794CB00002B/923